FLOW

A RECIPE FOR LIVING JOYFULLY

FLOW

A RECIPE FOR LIVING JOYFULLY

FINDING

LOVE

OVER

WORRY

KELLEY WOLF

Kelley Wolf
FLOW: Finding Love Over Worry

First Edition

ISBN 978-1-7779253-1-4

The definitions that form the book's epigram appear with grateful credit to Oxford Lexico.

Book design by Stephanie MacDougall
Editing by Lori Bamber
Publishing support by TSPA and Megan Williams

For Scott,
my love.

For Jackson, Miller and Lucy,
who show me that love is the answer.

And for my parents, Fred and Elaine,
who taught me that love always wins.

REC·I·PE:

a set of instructions for preparing a particular outcome including a list of the ingredients required.

FLOW /FLŌ:

undergo a permanent change of shape under stress, without melting.

FOREWORD

FOREWORD

I met Kelley Wolf in the parking lot of a restaurant in October 2013.

When you first see Kelley, it's easy to imagine her toasting glamorous friends at Soho House in West Hollywood or the Norwood Club in New York City. But when you get to know her, you learn very quickly that she is downhome Arkansas meets supernova, with a lot of love ninja mixed in.

That inimitable combination is exactly what I needed that weekend in Pismo Beach, California, at a Martha Beck workshop. We were both at a life coach training workshop, our first in-person meeting with people from all around the world.

At that time in my life, I was off kilter in my personal relationship and trying to find my place professionally after leaving a twenty-year career in television and media. I was nervous, as I knew no one and the group of women at the back of the long lineup were all talking and laughing. But as soon as I stepped in line, Kelley turned to me with a big smile and said, "Hi, I'm Kelley. Join us!"

That's Kelley—open, welcoming, genuine connection and good vibes. Her megawatt love ripples out to anyone and everything within a 360-degree radius.

We bonded over the next twenty-four hours, soul sisters re-united in a Marie Callender parking lot. That was exactly eight years ago this month, and I've since learned that Kelley is not only an extraordinary friend but an exceptional mom, wife, daughter, life coach and speaker.

She not only teaches FLOW, Finding Love Over Worry, she lives it!

Kelley has helped guide me through several Love vs. Worry moments, and damn, is she GOOD! She has done for me what she does so generously for everyone in her life—help us reconnect to Love and get back into the flow of our life, our true life. She does it effortlessly, with the forcefield of the love ninja she is. She is recharged by sharing what she has, spreading joy and being a beacon on the path of Love.

As Kelley says, "Each day is an opportunity to return to Love." In this book, she guides us through easy, practical exercises on how to do just that. It is a treasure map to a happier, more fulfilling life. I know this from my own experience: it works!

This is a heavy time for so many of us, wherever we are in the world. To meet the challenges ahead, we need Love, and we can do this, together.

October 31, 2021 Vancouver, BC, Canada

Libby Moore
Executive Coach, Speaker and former Chief of Staff to Oprah Winfrey

PROLOGUE

What if there were a recipe, a step-by-step way to minimize anxiety and frustration and cook up a better life? Doesn't that sound delicious!?

Well, here it is. I call it FLOW.

It all started with many coaching sessions in which my clients described their best moments as, "I was in flow," or "That is my flow."

I love looking for patterns in behavior and I began to track these conversations and the elements that were present in each of these experiences. I began to see, over and over, that the precursor to the flow state was FLOW:

Finding Love Over Worry.

Sometimes flow[1] captures us—a deep kiss, a wholehearted creative project—but the busier and more stressed we are, the more often we miss that call. My mission became helping my clients capture flow, and my study and research revealed that we tap into that otherwise elusive feeling when we first choose loving thoughts rather than worry thoughts.

If we feel flow while painting or cooking a meal, we have focused on our love of creating instead of worry and rumination. When we try skydiving, we choose our love of new experiences over our completely natural fear of jumping out of a plane.

Once I understood how powerful this simple framework is, I knew I had to share it with everyone I could. Now it's in your hands, the recipe to owning your peace—no matter what else is going on in your world right now.

It is easy to remember, easy to take with you and bite-size enough to do *all* the time.

I am so glad you are here. I use a touchstone phrase in my work: "I see you. I hear you. You are here, and you matter." I value your time, so I wrote this book to be accessible and to the point. The point? It's for all of us to truly live, not just survive.

Let's dig in and get you on the road to flow.

[1] The phrase "flow state" is attributed to the esteemed psychologist Mihaly Csikszentmihalyi. He and his colleague Jeanne Nakamura described its six attributes something like this:

1. We are focused entirely on the present moment.
2. Our actions and awareness merge.
3. We are unselfconscious.
4. We feel a sense of agency—we don't look to anyone else for approval.
5. We lose track of time.
6. We enjoy the experience no matter what the outcome.

A QUICK WORD ABOUT WORDS

Talking about the FLOW recipe and the flow state can be a little confusing, I know, so when I talk about the FLOW recipe, I use capital letters. When I talk about the state of flow, I use lowercase. When I talk about the four ingredients of FLOW as part of the recipe, I capitalize Finding, Love, Over and Worry. Otherwise, those words appear in lowercase.

Another word you'll come across a lot here is *love*. It's a word with a lot of baggage, and each one of us probably has a dozen unique-to-us definitions. I love chocolate chip cookies, I love nature, I love my children, I love my husband. I love myself. Each kind of love is radically different and what we mean when we talk about it varies from person to person.

When I talk about FLOW, however, Love has a precise meaning. It is the state of gratitude and everyday reverence that allows us to see people as they are—including ourselves—and the world as it is. Beautiful and broken and perfectly imperfect. Sacred. Worthy of our care. It is a state of presence, a way of being that honors this life we've been given and everything in it. It is acceptance of all that is, even as we work to make the world better.

That state, Love, is available to us at any time, using this very simple recipe. Shall we get cooking?

KELLEY'S ROAST CHICKEN RECIPE

KELLEY'S ROAST CHICKEN RECIPE

Nourishing food is so essential, and, for me, cooking is one of the easiest everyday ways to shift into flow. There was no way I could write this book without sharing some of my favorite recipes.

Cooking might not be your jam, but I implore you to get curious about the activities that stimulate flow for you. Even if you don't make them, let these recipes serve as a reminder to pull your passions to the front burner. Whatever your typical flow-inducing activities are, this is your gentle reminder to let them back into your life. Surrender to the magic of everyday activities that bring you into flow.

All that said, consider giving at least one of these recipes a try even if you don't usually cook. I wrote them as if we were in the kitchen together, cooking with a cup of tea and telling stories over the countertop. They are mostly simple and simply wonderful.

When great chefs are asked what their go-to comfort meal is, many of them say the same thing: a perfectly roasted chicken.

There is something about this meal that is reassuring, and always, always special. Maybe it reminds us of the generations that came before us and our astonishing human ability to make do with what we have.

Maybe it just tastes like home. My grandparents raised chickens on their land in rural Indiana. My grandmother lived in communion with the animals that were critical to her family's survival, from the hatching of the eggs to proudly setting her roasted chicken in the center of our family's supper table.

Modern life has disconnected us from the sources of our nourishment, which is one of the reasons I feel this recipe is an appropriate metaphor for FLOW. If we start each meal by acknowledging everyone who has contributed—including, in my case, my grandmother, the farmer who raised the chicken and the chicken—we will be in a state of gratitude. And gratitude will always lift us above the worries that otherwise distract us from Love.

INGREDIENTS

3 tablespoons butter, softened
2-3 tablespoons olive oil
2 lemons, cut in half
2 garlic cloves, cut in half, with skin on
10-15 sprigs of fresh thyme (or your favorite herb)
1-2 teaspoons of kosher salt
Pepper
1 onion sliced and drenched with olive oil
1 pound of carrots, cut in 1/4-inch-long slices
1 pound of red potatoes, cut into quarters
1 chicken

DIRECTIONS

Preheat your oven to 425 degrees.

Run the chicken under water and remove any leftover pin feathers. Then use a towel or paper towel to pat it dry inside and out.

Make sure you remove anything inside the cavity. (I learned this the hard way after discovering some roasted plastic in a dinner party chicken.)

Prepare the inside of the chicken. Put the garlic cloves and thyme inside the cavity, and then squeeze in the lemon juice. Stuff in the lemon pieces and sprinkle with salt and pepper. If the cavity will not close, tie it up with butcher string. Don't worry about technique—just do your best.

Massage the butter all over the chicken, adding a little olive oil if necessary to cover all the skin. Sprinkle generously with salt and pepper.

Place the sliced onions in the bottom of a sturdy roasting pan and place the chicken, breast side up, on top of the onion slices. (I have used a glass Pyrex dish, so if that is all you happen to have, use that.)

Now toss the potatoes and carrots in olive oil, salt and pepper and scatter around the chicken.

Roast for an hour to 90 minutes. Check at around one hour and stir the veggies to make sure they don't burn. When you poke a knife into the breast of the chicken and the liquid comes out clear, you are done.

To be extra sure, get a meat thermometer and look for the poultry marker.

Once the juices come out clear or the chicken has reached the recommended temperature on your probe, cover the whole pan with aluminum foil and let it sit for half an hour.

My grandmother used that time to make a cup of tea and do a crossword puzzle. Whenever I can, I honor her wisdom by using any downtime in cooking as recharging time for me. I am guilty of multitasking to the degree that I've ended up with a burnt chicken, which is why I love to use these between times for quiet me-time.

I serve this simple feast with a beautiful baguette and soft butter, a little finger bowl of sea salt on the side, and a simple green salad of arugula with olive oil, salt, pepper and lemon juice.

If you want a whole dinner party, skip ahead to the chocolate zucchini cake at the end of Chapter 7. Add the cake as a finale to this meal and your family and guests will be giddy with joy.

CHAPTER 1

THE FLOW FOUNDATION: THE 3M'S

No house will stand for long without a strong foundation built on stable land. Yet when buying or building a home, most of us want to leave the foundation to others and get straight to picking out the new lighting fixtures.

I get it! Lighting and throw cushions are way more fun than concrete.

However, when our aim is building a peaceful life, we must prioritize lasting change, with real power behind it. We want to be the house on the hill, not the mansion on a sinking swamp.

Before we get into the four pillars of FLOW, we must first establish our foundation, which I call the 3M's.

Munch, Move and Meditate.

You will be tempted to skip ahead. Don't. The reason so many of us shortchange ourselves is because this stuff seems obvious. We know we need to do it, and we will. If we have time.

Does this sound familiar?

Yet unless you are nourished, have felt your bones move under your skin today, and have a way to separate yourself from your thoughts, it can be almost impossible to reach a state of flow.

We snap and undermine the trust in our relationships by lashing out.

In Alcoholics Anonymous, there is a maxim known as HALT: Hungry, Angry, Lonely, Tired. People in recovery are taught that their sobriety depends on checking themselves for these states whenever they feel the intolerable discontent that can otherwise lead them back to drinking. Once these unmet needs are identified, the cure is usually simple. Feed yourself nourishing food. Allow yourself to feel your anger and ask it what it is trying to tell you about what you need to change in your life or what you value most. Check in with a friend, even if it is just a single text. If you're tired, have a nap. If you can't, give yourself a break—you cannot fix the world or yourself right now, but you can make it to bedtime.

In other words, these needs are basic, but they are also the foundation on which everything else rests. Making time to take care of them (and you) each day will make your life immeasurably better.

MUNCH

I am going to assume you are a human. Yes? Then there are a few things you need to survive. One of those things is food. I know, isn't this blowing your mind?

The truth is, so many people suffer through a big part of their day feeling frustrated and short-fused before they remember they haven't eaten. Then they grab whatever is nearest and easiest, which can make us feel even worse.

It is a cycle we must confront if we are to have FLOW become our default.

Let me put it this way. If you have not eaten and your partner leaves their shoes in the hallway and you trip on them, you will have a harder time Finding Love in your heart.

Eat. That is paramount.

A little while ago, one of my best friends accidentally put diesel fuel into her standard fuel car. She had to have a tow truck come to the gas station. A few weeks later, she was told the car may never work again. That was a big and very unfortunate snafu.

Our bodies are more adaptable than machines, which is why we often treat them so carelessly. But if we want to live well, to live in flow, we need good fuel. And we need it before the tank is empty. We cannot expect to operate at our fullest potential if we put junky fuel into our Maserati body or try to run on empty.

Each meal and snack is another opportunity to give yourself love. In fact, let me offer you a challenge: The next time you eat, sit down. Take the time to taste your food, give thanks and savor the gift of nourishment. The whole universe is conspiring to keep you alive and healthy, and it only needs your cooperation.

Thank you for this meal. Thank you to the seed, the water and the sun. Thank you to the farmer, the driver and the store for bringing it to my table. Thank you for this body to receive and enjoy such beautiful nourishment.

This might sound almost religious, but it doesn't have to be.

You can thank whatever and whoever you want. The goal is to return to a state of gratitude and remember that eating is a divine, sacred communion with the rest of the universe.

MOVE ≋

I must come clean about something. I am not a workout person. For many years, I even thought I didn't sweat because I didn't push hard enough to get to the sweating stage.

I was on the track team for a brief moment in high school, and if my competitor really wanted to win or their family was in the stands, I was happy to let them roll on by. I have very little competitive spirit around fitness-related endeavors.

A friend once told me she looks for someone she can "beat" to ride next to when she goes to a spin class because it motivates her. I am more inclined to want to out-bake you, but that is for another day.

We all have different ways to get our bodies moving, and mine has never been about competition or weight loss. My motivation came the hard way—through a devastating medical diagnosis.

Before I go into the diagnosis, I want to say that I believe the diagnosis, but not the prognosis. Remember this as we walk together: no one knows you better than you. When you listen, your body will talk to you. Your spirit will talk to you. As much as I would love to eavesdrop, you and only you will know your truths. This applies when we are diagnosed with any ailment. Believe the diagnosis but trust yourself, in communion with your medical advisors, when it comes to the prognosis.

I was diagnosed with something called Ehlers Danlos Syndrome, or EDS. It is a hyper-mobility disorder that presents in joint dislocations, hyper-flexibility and chronic pain. You are welcome to research more about it on your own, but for our purposes, I will just tell you that living in chronic pain is as devastating as you might imagine.

I went through all the stages of grief.

When you are told you may not be able to walk later in your life and that you will have to rely on a revolving door of doctors and interventions just to pick up your kids, it can take you out at the knees. I was terrified. Heartbroken. I felt defeated.

After I processed my feelings, I began to commit to small amounts of movement each day. I had once been strong and active, and I knew I could find my way back.

The most I could do some days was raise one hand at a time, up and down on the bed. Other days I could walk around the block. I slowly added distance, being careful not to push my body to a breaking point. (Or, in my case, a bending point.) I had to learn to ask my friends to slow down for me. Mostly, they were kind and willing, but I often walked alone.

Ah, the poetry in that.

Over time, I have come to crave my solitary morning walk. I don't feel whole without it. And the beauty of a morning walk is that I can do it almost anywhere.

Most days, I drag myself to the trail. Typically, the pain is toughest in the morning and I am far from peppy. Yet once I begin walking, my body responds and shows up with the energy I need to make the trek. I rely on habit to get me going; eventually my body picks up the call and carries me through.

It is not always easy. People are often shocked when I tell them how my body feels on the inside. My daily movement is a lifeline. You may not feel this level of intensity around movement, but we all need to move. Movement heals.

Humans are more sedentary than ever before, and not coincidentally, we report more physical and emotional pain than at any time in history. There is a proven correlation between our lack of movement and our lack of joy[2].

I know I can feel my thoughts shift when I move. Stress is lowered. Love is heightened.

If you want more flow in your life, commit to movement each day. Notice how you feel before and after, even if you start by just lifting your arms off your bed as I did.

Over time, you may wish to increase the time you devote to this practice. But give yourself permission to start small. If you told me when I started that I would hike mountains every single day without struggle, I would have laughed.

I am proof of the power of putting one foot in from of the other and—starting.

Just start.

[2] Zhang, Z., Chen, W. A Systematic Review of the Relationship Between Physical Activity and Happiness. *J Happiness Stud 20*, 1305–1322 (2019). https://doi.org/10.1007/s10902-018-9976-0

MEDITATE

I know. If someone suggests you try meditation just one more time!

I hear you.

Before you move on, though, we should probably both admit that we know that meditation comes highly recommended because it makes life better for almost everyone who does it. Even more importantly, I am here to tell you that you do not have to find time you don't have, sit on the floor and torture yourself. Incorporating meditation into your life can be easy and convenient.

Yes, I said it, and I'm about to prove it.

When my oldest son was six months old, I decided to train in transcendental meditation. The cornerstones of TM are meditating twice a day for twenty minutes, using a mantra given to you by your teacher.

Nothing felt harder.

I argued with my teacher about the difficulty of doing this with an infant. I felt my alone time was the most precious asset I had and should be spent watching TV, of course.

His only response was, "I have five kids."

Boo.

I finished the course and came to a place where I appreciated the benefits of TM's approach. However, I have made some adaptations over the years. I now have three kids, two dogs, a podcast and a thriving career. The little alone time I had back then has become non-existent.

I could recommend waking up early, staying up late or just doing the practice while chaos happens around you, but those methods didn't work for me.

What worked for me was what I started calling "Wash the Face."

I named tasks I was doing as I was doing them: Wash the dishes, pack the lunches, walk the dogs.

When I repeated the description of the task I was doing in my head, my mind wandered into Clutterville less. It became a form of mindfulness meditation.

Once I mastered the "wash the face" method of meditation, I started integrating repetition of my TM mantra into moments throughout my day. If I could grab two minutes to sit, I would take them, repeating my mantra and taking deep breaths. If I add up all the times I now do this in a day, it often equals the forty minutes that conventional TM protocol requires. But unlike the TM protocol, it's possible to do even in a life that's already beautifully full.

Meditation doesn't have to be complicated. (We may need to rebrand it as *Quiet Time* or *Sitting Time.*) The goal is just to quiet your mind, to prevent being captured by looped thoughts or tripping over mental clutter. Remember, the benefits start as soon as you see your thoughts as separate from yourself. All you really must do is practice managing your attention for a few minutes today and then again tomorrow. And then the day after that. You can't do this wrong if you do it.

For me, it is a bit like having a sink full of dirty pots and pans. I can leave it like that, but I feel so much better when I take a few minutes to wash them.

The same goes for our minds. Cleaning out the clutter does not mean more clutter won't come. It means you get in a rhythm, taking care of your mind just as you take care of your kitchen. And that means more room to breathe—more room to flow.

LET'S REVIEW

Munch: You know who you are: you get to 2 PM and realize you've had only coffee and a banana. Or you consistently reach for highly processed rather than whole foods because processed foods come in handy snack packs. Of course, if this is the only food available, eat it—but make a shift when you can.

Your challenge: get in the habit of putting the right fuel into your body at the right times. If you don't, know that your experience of the world will be filtered through your body's urgent cries for quality fuel, which feel just like anxiety and frustration.

When things are crazy and you can't eat well, don't beat yourself up—grab a banana and some walnuts and move on.

Move: We are the most sedentary versions of humans since the beginning of time. We also report high prevalence of anxiety and depression[3]. Do we see the possible correlation?

Your challenge: If you love a hardcore workout class, then get after it, by all means!!! If you need a slower pace, I can promise you there is a road just outside your door waiting to feel your feet.

[3] Saloni Dattani, Hannah Ritchie and Max Roser (2021) - "Mental Health." Published online at OurWorldInData.org. https://ourworldindata.org/mental-health

I once walked around a sofa a hundred times in a hotel room with sleeping babies. You can do this. You can find big and small ways to start moving your body. Before you know it, it will be a habit you cannot live without.

Meditate: Our mind is our greatest asset—and can also be our greatest enemy. Learning to manage your mind's habit of wandering and worrying will be the *thing,* I promise.

When I say I trained in transcendental meditation (I will piss people off here), I mean I hired and paid a teacher to work with me, which is how TM works. I am glad I took the training—I think I did it to confirm we do not need to pay anyone for this ancient gift.

Your challenge: Here are my favorite ways to wet your meditation whistle, FLOW-style.

Wash the Hair

This is a method I created to save myself while raising three small children, when the only place I was alone was the shower. Can you relate?

I would turn on the water and resist the urge to go over my to-do list. Instead, I would say, "Wash the hair." "Shave the legs." "Soap the body."

You get my point. I said, out loud, the things I was doing, and it moved my mind towards a place of presence and mindfulness.

"Wash the dishes." "Fold the laundry."

Try it. You will see that your thoughts begin to slow down; you'll feel sensations like peace, presence and gratitude.

The Five-Minute Method

Everyone has five minutes somewhere in their day. Aim for twenty and you're more likely to talk yourself out of it, but a five-minute commitment is hard to argue with.

Set a timer, sit quietly and take deep breaths.

Optional twist: If you wish, you may use a mantra. Search online to find one that speaks to you and then say it over and over as you sit and breathe.

The Name It Method

I use this as a walking meditation. While I am walking, if I find my mind playing ping pong, I start to name the things I see—tree, pink flower, green worm, etc.

This method is also a great cognitive-behavioral technique to stop anxiety from rising. If I feel myself getting anxious, I name things I see around me. After I have named a few items, I begin to come back to the present moment. Except in those rare moments of our lives when we experience trauma, we are *always* safe in the present moment.

When we are in an acute anxiety attack, our brain receives signals that it identifies as immediate danger. Our body responds with a hormonal surge that induces fight, flight or freeze mode. We may sweat, shake or feel flushed.

Our bodies are doing their jobs. Our bodies and minds are not the enemy, and we are not damaged goods. These are survival responses meant to save our lives. However, if you are not in imminent danger, try taking three deep breaths and then using the name-it method to get your heart rate down and your mind focused on your present moment of safety. Repeat the mantra:

"I am safe, this is not real.

I am safe, this is not real.

I am safe. I am safe. I am safe."

Let's talk briefly about your phone because I know there are many great meditation apps. If screens are not one of your drugs of choice, you might get away with turning on "do not disturb" before you start any meditation practice.

If you aren't using your phone to meditate, put it in another room. The energy it has is extraordinary. Whether it is an unanswered text or the pull of a social media conversation, that energy stands between you and your peace. If you are using an app or your phone's timer, I suggest putting it a few feet away from you. Also, if your mom hasn't told you, then I will. *Do not* look at your phone first thing in the morning. At a minimum, wait ten minutes after waking. Ideally, wait an hour.

Setting your morning up for peace sets your day up for peace. As soon as you look at your phone, you are opening up to problems that need solutions. If this happens early in the morning, you probably will not yet have the clarity to respond well to them. The result is an immediate zap of anxiety.

For those early moments, the only solution you should be focusing on is Finding and settling into your peace. Doing so will equip you with the tools and energy you need to meet the rest of the day.

A final word on your FLOW foundation: all of this assumes that you prioritize getting enough sleep each night. If you don't know how much sleep is enough for you, aim for eight hours. To "prioritize" means to cancel appointments if you need to, to bring your kids to school late and tell the teachers you all had to catch up on your sleep, even to call in sick if you had a bout of insomnia the night before.

I am optimistic that we are seeing the light on sleep. We made it the bad guy for many years, but as the research comes out, we are all waking up to the immense benefits of a good night's rest. Waking up, get it?

When you don't get enough sleep, acknowledge that the quality of your day will be undermined by the shortage, depending on your tolerance level[4], just as it would be if you were ill. Recognize that you may be short-tempered and reactive. Most things will feel more difficult when you are sleep deprived. Ultimately, give yourself some slack if you have not had good rest.

The Dalai Lama once said that the very best meditation is sleep. If you struggle to get enough, like so many of us, and find ten minutes of you-time, a combo nap-meditation may be magic.

[4] Many people report that this is one of the first things to change in midlife—we feel much worse when we don't get enough sleep, even if we're only short-changed by half an hour. https://www.sciencedirect.com/science/article/abs/pii/S0378512210004573

Get comfortable and make your mantra "rest." Breathe deeply and repeat it over and over, instructing your unconscious to let it all go for a bit. Feel rest moving through your body, from your toes to the top of your scalp.

Look at that! You just did a meditation by going to bed, and you will be amazed at how much brighter the world looks afterward.

NUT BUTTER BALLS

I chose this recipe for this chapter because I keep these in my fridge *all* the time. When I am in a hurry, when I have forgotten to eat, when I need a little pick-me-up, these are the perfect remedy. You could do the "wash the hair" meditation while you make this ... scoop the peanut butter, turn on the mixer. Or you can just make them! That is an option too. Enjoy!

INGREDIENTS

1 cup oats
2/3 cup shredded coconut
1/2 cup nut butter of your choice (I love peanut butter)
1/3 cup honey
1/2 teaspoon vanilla extract (optional)
1/2 cup dried cranberries (or any dried fruit)
1/2 cup pumpkin seeds (or other seeds)
Chocolate chips (optional)

DIRECTIONS

Mix all ingredients together using a high-speed blender if you have one, or your hands if you don't. Add or subtract ingredients to your taste.

Roll into balls and keep in the fridge for easy grab-and-go nourishment.

CHAPTER 2

WHAT THE F...LOW—
WHERE DID THIS COME FROM?

My first birth, with our son Jack, was relatively easy—I was able to have a natural birth and a peaceful postpartum experience. My second, with Miller, was much more traumatic. He was crowning and then decided to turn around and go back through the birth canal and lay sideways. It is called transversing. If you know Miller now, you know how he loves a good flip at the party. He was staying on brand. We had to be rushed to a c-section; luckily, we all made it out alive. I will be forever grateful for the quick thinking of my doctor, Howie Mandel and all the nurses at Cedar Sinai. (And no, not that Howie Mandel.)

Lucy came seventeen months after Miller, and her birth was a planned c-section. Much less traumatic, but it was still very hard on my body, and I did not get the magical hormone oxytocin[5] that I later learned is released during natural birth.

[5] Doctors now often administer oxytocin to c-section moms. Science is pretty amazing! ZHANG, H., LIU, H., LUO, S. et al. Oxytocin use in trial of labor after cesarean and its relationship with risk of uterine rupture in women with one previous cesarean section: a meta-analysis of observational studies. BMC Pregnancy Childbirth 21, 11 (2021). https://doi.org/10.1186/s12884-020-03440-7

After Lucy was born, I was in a lot of pain, my c-section incision was reopening, and my body felt wrecked. We didn't know it at the time, but EDS makes it hard for your tissue to come back together after surgery. Without getting into the gory details, when this happens, the wound can't be re-stitched due to the high risk of infection. Instead, you must just wait, with an open wound, until it heals naturally.

My husband Scott was my nurse. Each day he would do the work of cleaning and packing my incision. He never complained and he never made me feel like I was a burden. It was one of many profound experiences of love I have felt in my life, and I will be forever grateful for his steadfast love for me and for our children. You might imagine these would be hard days, and they were, but something was brewing that would prove to be the most harrowing time of my life.

I had what is called a postpartum breakdown; I became obsessively suicidal and almost comatose.

More than once, I looked at Scott and said, "Honey, don't you get it? You will have a much better life without me. You can find a great woman to help you raise the kids, and everyone will be better for it."

It made perfect sense to me, and I could not understand why no one else could see my rationale. I was put on a suicide watch, and all the dangerous items were carefully removed from our home.

The weeks and months that followed were a kind of hell I would not wish on any human. I felt utterly alone, scared, embarrassed, in pain and done. I felt done. Didn't women die in childbirth? Why did the universe refuse me this gift?

Finally, one day, I called a dear friend, Libby Moore. I speak of this moment often, and you may have heard it on my podcast or at a talk, but it bears repeating yet again because it possibly saved my life. Libby is the best coach and consultant I know. She was also Oprah Winfrey's chief of staff for eleven years—this story will make more sense when you have that piece of information.

I called Libby from the depths of my despair.

She said, "May I share a story with you?"

When Libby offers a story, you would have to be a damn fool to turn it down. Libby's stories are *good!*

Libby continued, "One day, I was in my office at Harpo. I was drowning in work. I was in a spiral."

Maya Angelou (I know, this is Libby's life) called and noticed Libby didn't seem like herself. She asked if she was okay. After hearing a bit about how she was feeling, Dr. Angelou asked her to go outside and stare at the tree in front of the Harpo building "long enough to see it." She suggested this act would bring Libby back home to herself.

Libby said, "Kelley, can you go outside and look at a tree? I mean, look at it until you see it?"

I am pretty sure that if this request had not originated with the great Dr. Angelou, I would have hung up. I was in no space for random tree staring. But I agreed to do it.

We hung up, and I held my gut packing (sorry guys) together and found a tree. I purposely found the biggest and oldest-looking tree on our overpopulated street in Los Angeles. I sat down in front of the tree and began to stare. I do not know how long I was there, but my body ached from sitting, so it was quite a while.

Then. Something. Happened.

I heard a bird chirp.

I smelled car exhaust. (This was LA, after all.)

I saw the bark of the tree, the green of the grass.

Why is this noteworthy? Because I had not seen, heard, felt or experienced anything but terror in months. I am sure the world had continued to turn, but not in my head. In my mind, I had lived in constant fear and foreboding.

I was ecstatic. I felt hope for the first time since the breakdown. Actual hope. Maybe, just maybe, I was going to be okay. I could see a small glimmer of light at the end of this horrific tunnel of depression.

I put my arms around the tree. I thanked her for watching over my house. I thanked her for watching over all the other mothers before me who had felt despair. I thanked her for this glimpse at life.

I could not stop crying. This time, though, I cried tears of joy. That night was the first time I heard Lucy's little coos. I heard the boys laughing. I could taste my food and hear the music playing. The cacophony of despair became quieter in my mind. I was slowly coming back to my body.

The next morning, I woke at dawn to feed Lucy. As soon as I put her back in her bed, I threw on my shoes because I could not wait to go back and look at my tree.

This, I vowed, would be my daily ritual. I would spend each morning with my tree, and it would help to bring me back to life. I threw open the door, but something was wrong. I stopped dead in my tracks. I could not believe what I was seeing.

My tree. My savior. My dearest—

had fallen.

You read that right. The tree I chose. The tree that woke me up. The biggest, oldest tree on our block had fallen.

I looked around for the unlikely LA tornado. Maybe lightning? Maybe a rogue gust of wind that targeted only *my* tree?

I could not find the cause and my mind jumped to the worst-case scenario. As it does when we are in that space, right? Was this a sign that I should just give up, give in? If this tree could not withstand the challenges of the world, what chance did I have?

I dropped to my knees and put my hands over my mouth to muffle the scream that was coming, but something else happened. I was flooded with a powerful sense of peace. If there is a time when I could claim to hear the voice of God, this was it. I am not religious, but I believe in a higher power, something we cannot see that provides a sense of love and peace.

That voice said:

"Your power will never come from something outside of you. You hold the keys to your peace, and you are the gatekeeper of your happiness. You are whole and complete, just as you are. You are made from love. You are love."

Now let me be clear. I did not magically feel better. The road ahead would be long and hard, but something essential had changed. I knew something I had never known. Like Dorothy and Harry Potter and Luke Skywalker—it was in *me* all along. The power to transcend. The power to heal. The power to change.

It is in *you*. And it is guided by one, ever-abiding light—Love.

DAD'S PECAN PIE

Making this pie for my dad is an act of love performed in our home each year. He has learned to make it himself but we insist on making it for him. It is an admirable pie, but it is the joy it brings to his life that is the real winner.

If I have the energy, I love to make a full butter crust—I love Ina Garten's pie crust recipe. And there is no shame in a delicious Marie Callender frozen crust from your grocer.

This is a simple recipe you can make in one bowl in a few minutes and the payoff is pretty special.

Are you seeing a theme here? Simple + loving = magic.

INGREDIENTS

One pie crust (Your own or store-bought)
1 cup brown sugar
1 cup white corn syrup
1 tsp vanilla
3 eggs, beaten
6 tablespoons melted butter
1/2-1 teaspoon Kosher salt
2-3 cups pecans

DIRECTIONS

Mix all ingredients in a bowl or a standing mixer. Mix until combined and pour into a prepared (uncooked) pie shell. Place the pecans on top and use the back of a spatula or your hand to gently press them into the delicious mix. Lick your fingers.

I like to put this on a cookie sheet in case a little bubbles over because I have had the pleasure of cleaning hardened corn syrup mix off the bottom of my oven. Do as I say, not as I do.

Bake for 40 to 50 minutes. When there is only a little jiggle, it is finished. If your crust is burning and your filling is still jiggling, place aluminum foil over it.

I love to serve this with homemade whipped cream with a splash of bourbon, or a really good vanilla ice cream.

Love you, Dad.

CHAPTER 3
LIVING THAT RUBBER MIND LIFE

My goal in writing this book is to give you the FLOW recipe so that you can live in a state of flow more often.

I want you to know you have the power to do so.

I want you to know you can make your life more joyful.

It will all start with your mindset.

I know. "Mindset" gets used more often and more roughly than a hacky sack at a Grateful Dead reunion. Let me break down what I mean and tell you why it's doable, no matter where you are right now.

As I mentioned earlier, our brains are plastic. It means that our brains can rewire and rewire, over and over, based on the information and patterns we input. "Pattern" is the most important word here. Our brains love patterns! They love to know what the next step is. This preference is why we create habits, like driving to work the same way, or waking up and making a coffee before anything else. Do you tend to do the same nighttime routine every night? This is a habit. Whatever you do repeatedly becomes your brain's default. When we understand the power of repetition, we can apply behaviors like FLOW and allow them to become default functions.

Think of your mindset like a clock. Just as you can set an alarm on your clock, you can set your mind to help you heal and live a more joyful life. In the case of the clock, you just push the right buttons in the correct order—in the case of your mind, if you cycle through the relevant behaviors enough, it will set itself!

Let me say here that, although I was the president of the science club in fifth grade, I'm not a scientist. I do love a good hypothesis, though, and one of the most fascinating lectures I heard while getting my clinical psychology degree was about myelin.

Myelin is a white, fatty substance in our brains. Throughout our lives, but especially as we go through adolescence and discover ways to avoid death, myelin hardwires into pathways.

Myelin was very helpful in the Paleolithic era. (My dad is an archeologist, so yes, I do say words like Paleolithic.) These were the days of early humans, when a bad berry could kill you and the path down by the river was where the tigers lived. It was crucial to hardwire patterns that made survival more likely. Our ancestors didn't often live beyond the age of thirty-three, which is another reason to work on the old fear-based mindset—we are likely to have it for a while.

Things have changed since the times of early humans. Unless you are reading this in the Serengeti, and I sincerely hope you are because it is my favorite place on earth, you may be happy to hear you are no longer in danger of being hunted by a giant cat when you step outside.

Because we no longer need to use as much of our brains for survival, we can rewire them for changes in mindset.

I believe this is a critical, world-changing step in human evolution. It makes sense that the absence of daily threats to our survival means we can feel safe and content almost all the time, doesn't it?

Yet even as we live through the easiest of lifetimes, as measured by world violence and access to goods, services and modern medicine, we are unsatisfied and chronically anxious. We may fabricate danger when there is none. We have an operating system that was programmed by our ancestors and that just can't believe we can be at peace and live long happy lives.

Changing our mindset reprograms that ancient, outdated operating system.

Your mind can change. But—it needs your help, and it requires a strategy. I will provide the strategy; your part is incorporating it into your daily routine.

Together, we can make flow.

Because *when your mind changes, your life changes.*

FOOLPROOF BREAD

How is this possible? Bread is the most daunting of all the baked goods. Right?! Wrong. Just like learning your brain is plastic and can change, this recipe will change your mind about bread.

This no-knead bread recipe is everywhere on the Internet but this particular version is inspired by one in *The New Artisan Bread in 5 Minutes a Day* by Jeff Hertzberg M.D. and Zoe Francois. I couldn't recommend this book more.

I also call this Meditation Bread because making bread is a great meditation!

INGREDIENTS

3 cups barely warm water
2 tablespoons granulated yeast
1 1/2 tablespoons kosher salt (or any other coarse salt)
6 1/2 cups unsifted, unbleached all-purpose flour
2 tablespoons butter or olive oil (optional)

DIRECTIONS

Preparing Your Dough

Run your water until it feels warm but not hot to your elbow (a grandma trick!) and pour 3 cups into a large bowl.

Add the yeast.

Add the flour and salt with dry measuring utensils. (In other words, don't use a measuring cup meant for liquids.) Scrape off the top so they aren't heaped but do not press down.

If you're ready for an arm workout, use a wooden spoon to combine the ingredients. If not, you could also use a dough hook on your mixer or a large food processor. You're finished when all your flour is wet. If your muscles wear out before this happens, don't be afraid to wet your hands and get in there.

Cover loosely. (Cover tightly and you may get a small explosion, and nobody needs that kind of surprise.)

Let the dough rise at room temperature until it gets flat on the top, about two hours depending on how warm your home is and how warm your water was. Letting it rise for up to five hours is also fine.

It's now ready for baking, but it gets even easier to work with after it is refrigerated for a bit.

When You're Ready to Bake

Grease your loaf tin, cookie tray or whatever you wish to bake with. (Some of my friends insist on using their Dutch ovens—it's hard to go wrong here.)

Sprinkle your dough with flour. Grab a grapefruit-sized bit of dough and cut it off with a serrated knife.

Sprinkle a bit more flour on the bit you're working with to make it less sticky. Lucy loves to toss this ball from one floured hand to the next—we call it "pat the baby butt."

Gently stretch the top of the ball around to the bottom on all four sides, turning it a quarter-turn as you go. The bottom may now look a bit like a lumpy flower, but it will sort itself out later. The top should look like a loaf. Don't get fancy—this part should take less than a minute. You will now have a cute little "boule" shape. Boule is French for ball! I just figured that out.

Let your loaf rise for 40 minutes. It may not expand a lot, which is fine.

20 minutes before baking, preheat the oven to 450 F. Place an empty broiler tray anywhere in the oven that won't get in the way of the rising bread and pour in a cup of hot tap water when you're ready to bake.

Sprinkle the loaf with flour again and use a serrated knife to slash a ¼-inch-deep cross, diagonal lines, or a tic-tac-toe pattern on top. This will make you feel like a professional baker when the bread is baked.

After 20 minutes, you're ready to bake even if your oven isn't at 450 F yet. For a slightly less tooth-jarring crust, now is the time to use your optional butter or olive oil—just rub it gently onto the top of the loaf. A sprinkle of salt or rosemary wouldn't go wildly amiss.

Bake for about 30 minutes.

Store the rest of the dough in the fridge, loosely covered, for up to 14 days. It gets even better, with a slightly sourdough-like taste. You can have a fresh boule every night of the week. If that doesn't bring you joy, I don't know what will.

CHAPTER 4

F IS FOR FINDING—AND OTHER LESSONS FROM SESAME STREET

I am pretty sure the creators of Sesame Street were among the enlightened ones. They carried messages of hope and love through simple ideas.

Like FLOW—simple. Once you understand the mechanisms, you can apply them in every moment of your life until ... *boom* ... your plastic mind defaults to choosing Love over Worry.

Each letter in FLOW stands for an essential part of your mindset strategy. Let's start with the letter F. I do love other words that start with the letter F, but today we will be talking about Finding. Finding is where we become the observer of our thoughts. Do not worry. I am not tripping on acid, although I did one time at the Grand Canyon. I left the campsite to tie up our trash and ended up getting lost. Well, not lost, but tripping lost. Instead of walking any further, I decided to lay on the dirt and look at the stars. That night was a perfect example of becoming an observer.

In this case, you do not need drugs, but this will still seem... trippy.

The first thing I'd like you to observe is that our thoughts are not real.

Thoughts are thoughts. They do not hold water like a cup or have four legs like a dog. Thoughts can feel real, but they are not.

When I was going through postpartum depression, my thoughts told me the world around me was dangerous and cruel. One time I remember clearly, I was sitting under a tree in my backyard, in a suburb of Los Angeles. The sun was shining and my loving family was nearby. Any rational witness would be shocked to learn I felt nothing but fear and despair.

Your thoughts are powerful. They are convincing, and the more you focus on a particular line of thinking, the truer it feels. Cue—myelin. Myelin is like the ruts in a dirt road. If you drive over them enough times, they become a perfect conduit for your tires. If you decide to drive outside of the rut and make a new one, staying in it each time, it will eventually become the dominant rut. Dirt and water will fill the old rut and it soon won't even be visible.

Myelin is the same. Whatever you repeat will become hard-wired. Good or bad.

Here is a silly but typical example. I used to pass the same mom every day as I dropped my kids off at school. Let's call her Debbie. Now, remember, I grew up in the South. You wave or smile at every car you pass, making a conscious effort to make eye contact with the other driver to show your human solidarity. That could be a whole other book on how to become a chronic people-pleaser. But in this story, I waved or smiled at Debbie from my car each day, and not once did she wave or smile back. I didn't know her outside of the pick-up line, but man, did I create a character for Debbie. She was a huge stinker who thought she was better than me. Better than everybody, for that matter. She was rude. She was entitled. She was—not my people.

You know what I am talking about. We have all done this. I had created such a story that Debbie didn't stand a chance when we were seated next to each other at a school concert. I thought, what are the odds of being seated next to the rudest mom in the school?

I bet you know where this is headed. I introduced myself to Debbie like the Southern girl I am, and she acted like the loveliest person in the world. As if I'm falling for that. Then, as we watched the school performance, she kept asking me about details on the stage. What was in the corner? Was that Trevor from first grade?

She whispered, "I have the worst long-distance vision, even with my glasses."

Ugh. I felt like such an ass. Here I was creating stories in my mind that had much more to do with my need to be liked and my old codependence than it did with any truth about Debbie.

We think thousands and thousands of untrue, partially true or unprovable thoughts each day. To live in flow, we need to get in the habit of watching out for thoughts that hold us back from creating the life we want.

We need to challenge our assumptions and notice when we are creating a story.

When we become an observer, we start by noticing our thoughts as thoughts. It seems simple enough, but you will be surprised how often you believe your thoughts even though there is just no way you could know if they are true.

Another friend of mine has a maxim she turns to whenever she or her children start to worry: "It's too early to worry." She follows that up with, "We don't have enough information yet. Let's do some research." That flips them all into curiosity without shutting down possibility. Abraham Lincoln once said, "I don't like that man. I must get to know him better."

I have been aware of this phenomenon for ten years. Yet remembering to observe my thoughts is still one of my most difficult and vital daily tasks. That's okay. It is not our level of skill at this process that makes our life better, but the process itself. If you are trying, you are benefiting. The sheer recognition of thoughts as thoughts is a profound step towards a more peaceful life.

Now that we know thoughts are not real, our next job is to notice our worry thoughts. Worry thoughts are repeated, looping thoughts that cause suffering and discomfort.

An important note: as we work through the FLOW recipe, it is crucial to delineate worry from emotions like anger, fear, frustration and envy once again. One of these things is not like the other, and it is worry. Your feelings are crucial to your life, your healing and your evolution. Worry? Not so much.

Worry is seductive because it can feel like we are doing something even (especially) when we know we are worrying about something outside of our control. It can also feel like caring.

Consider watching the news and hearing a story about something that happened thousands of miles away from your home. You begin to worry about the possibility of this happening in your future or about the people in the news story in the way you would if this were your family member. You may begin to feel foreboding and maybe fear.

Worry is neither caring nor constructive. It drains our energy, making us less likely to do anything productive to change our situation. It saps our ability to problem-solve, which is highly problematic in real crises. In a true crisis, we need clear-headed action. Worry too often becomes a placeholder for doing anything at all.

Difficult emotions like envy and anger are beneficial to our growth. They should not be brushed away and ignored—they are flags that our psyche sends up to get our attention and convince us to look within. They are an essential part of our human experience. Ignoring our emotions can lead to dangerous outcomes like addiction and self-sabotage.

Emotions need our attention. The importance of allowing ourselves to feel and move through our emotions is why we must understand that worry is not an emotion. It is a thought loop, usually based on false or unprovable beliefs, created by a fixation on a possible negative outcome.

Here are a few common worry-thought-loop themes I hear from my friends, my clients and myself:

I am fat.
I am lazy.
Everyone else has done more than me.
I will never get this done.
I will be alone forever.
It is too late for me.
I am too young to do x.

I am too old to do x.
I drink too much.
I am always distracted.
I'm too impatient with my kids.
I am a bad mother.
I am a bad father.

These are just a few of the greatest hits. Have you ever rolled around in any of these? I know I have!

One of the most significant issues with worry loops is they lack action. They are like those dirty pots and pans. They serve no purpose other than to annoy you and stink up the place. The magic comes when we do the dishes. The magic comes when we act. That will come later in the book!

For now, just notice. Lean into observation. Get curious about your thoughts. That is the essence of Finding. A big part of this process is awareness. It will shock you how often you find you are in a worry loop, just going on about your business with no awareness of the rollercoaster your mind is on.

Let's get off the Rocket of Doom ride and watch it go by. Observe. Breathe in. Breathe out. Observe again.

Now repeat. I warned you; we have lots of thoughts!

I recently had a client ask me, with a gasp, "Do I have to do this all day?!"

Yes!!

Until—you don't. Remember, the only way to rewire that plastic pathway is to do something else repetitively. In this case, you will be repeating the observation of your thoughts until your brain no longer needs the reminder.

Find will be your default, and you will begin to sidestep that worry pothole.

Imagine the freedom that waits ahead for you!

24-HOUR PORK ROAST

This chapter deserves slow food because the process of Finding is a slow burn. You will need to make and take time to access and train this ability.

Like the rewards of observing your thoughts, this meal is worth the wait. I make it for special occasions or holidays. It is an easy recipe, but it seems daunting and it takes time. Sound familiar?

The reward is great, my friend. Enjoy!

I adapted this recipe from *The Slow Mediterranean Kitchen: Recipes for a Passionate Cook* by Paula Wolfert. Her carrots with olives recipe is also dynamite!

INGREDIENTS

One 6- to 7-pound bone-in fresh pork picnic shoulder roast with skin on
2 heads of garlic
1 tablespoon coarse sea salt
1 teaspoon freshly ground pepper
1 1/2 teaspoons dried oregano or marjoram
1 teaspoon dried thyme
2 large onions, sliced thin
4 carrots, sliced
A half-cup oloroso sherry
4 cups chicken stock
Crushed hot red pepper flakes
1 1/2 teaspoons top-quality sherry vinegar or balsamic vinegar

DIRECTIONS

Heat your oven to 450 F.

Score the skin of the roast like a ham, making deep crosscuts about an inch apart.

Crush the garlic with the salt, pepper, oregano and thyme. Massage all over the roast.

Put the roast on a rack in an oiled, shallow roasting pan, skin up, and roast for 45 minutes. It should be a deep golden-brown color.

Put the onion and carrot slices around the pork along with

half the sherry and stock. Add about a 1/4 teaspoon of hot pepper flakes, or to taste.

Lower the oven temperature to 180 F and roast about 12 hours, basting a couple of times. The center of the meat should reach 170 to 175 F. If it reaches that temperature in less than 12 hours, lower the oven temperature to 160 F while you prepare whatever sides you wish to serve. You can even leave it in the oven for up to 24 hours if that is more convenient.

Half an hour before dinner, put the roast on your carving board. Tent it with foil and a towel and put it in a warm place.

Add the rest of the sherry and stock to the pan over heat. Bring the liquid to a boil, scraping up the delectable, browned morsels from the bottom of the pan, until you have about a cup of "jus." Strain into a bowl or gravy boat, pressing on the vegetables. Skim off as much fat as you'd prefer, add the vinegar, and check to see if you need more salt and pepper.

Cut the pork skin into thick strips, slice the roast across the grain and arrange it all on your platter. Pour the pan juices over the meat. I serve this with scalloped potatoes (I love Julia Child's Gratin Dauphinois) and simple roasted brussels sprouts.

Give yourself and your people some scrumptious food love.

CHAPTER 5
L IS FOR LOVE

Can you feel it?

Welcome to the land of Love.

Remember when the tree fell, and the voice reminded me of the love that lives in me? The love that lives in you?

That love is the current under all calm. It is the current and the calm. It is the scaffolding of the beautiful life you are creating.

Love exists even when you cannot feel it. It is an ever-abiding, patient friend who will always have a room waiting for you.

The Beatles; Martin Luther King, Jr.; Gandhi; Rumi; Mother Teresa; Jesus—they all knew this. Their words try to break through our deep resistance to this simple truth.

Love is the answer.

How can it be so simple? It can't, right? At least that is what our fear is committed to believing, so we can stay safely stuck in our caves even if there is nothing there but suffering.

Love would be too simple.

One of the most elusive concepts I have ever come across is self-love. To be clear, I'm talking about the kind of self-love that is not about self-care or outward appearances but is much, much deeper. It is the kind of self-love that always picks up the phone, no matter how much or how little you call, and it always says yes. In recent years, we have been inundated with self-love advice. Yet when we see a meme or a video or a friend saying, "The key is self-love," we nod and are left wondering how to go about it. What does it mean?

Do we look in the mirror and say, "I love you"? Do we buy ourselves roses?

The reality is that self-love is a journey, not a light switch. Learning to see ourselves as worthy of love is hard, to say the least.

It turns out we are our own worst enemies. Negative self-talk is as common as humidity in Florida. Learning to turn off the voice that says, "You are such an idiot!" or "Who do you think you are?" takes time, attention and practice.

I had the lucky or unlucky experience of being filmed on a reality show for five months when I was twenty-two years old. Five months of being filmed while wearing a microphone is a surreal experience. When you wear a microphone all day, you become acutely aware of the things you say. Especially to yourself! I was shocked at how many times I spoke to myself. Sometimes it was encouraging things like, "You've got this," and, "You can do it." But more often, it was, "You idiot!" "That was stupid," and "You look horrible." I remember thinking, "Would I let someone else talk to me like this?"

No!

The abuse we direct at ourselves is often the worst abuse we experience. If you call yourself an idiot every day for forty years, you will undoubtedly feel like an idiot. You will live your life in a way that apologizes for this obvious shortcoming. When good things come toward you, you will respond with shame. "I don't deserve it." "This can't last." "They don't really know me."

To begin the journey of self-love, we must start with our internal dialogue.

Let's start with that inner critic. Maybe it has a favorite insult about how you should be ashamed of your body, your laugh, your parenting. If it were the voice of an actual person, we would swiftly remove them from our circle. Yet here they are, in our minds and our hearts each day.

As you begin to observe the inner critic, take a moment and recall your most recent self-inflicted insult. Can you hear it? Okay, that's the one.

Now, let us turn the critic into a guest at our table, a rude and unwelcome guest.

First, acknowledge its existence: "Ah, it's you again. I see you."

Next, ask it to leave for now: "Would you kindly run an errand for me? You can come back, but I need a minute alone."

It will come back. It always comes back. But this is your chance to invite Love over for coffee. Quick. Get Love to the table because you may only have a few minutes.

While you are alone with Love, let it remind you of all the beautiful things about you: your strong, capable arms that hold your babies, your adorable laugh, your perfect scrambled eggs. Let it get embarrassing—let Love go on and on. Until you are red in the face. When the critic returns, it will feel so out of place it will likely turn tail and leave.

Love will tell you that you are so much more than the sum of your parts. You were perfectly created to manifest your special magic. You cannot be replicated, and you cannot be replaced. *You are made of Love.* You are the one and only beautiful you.

Love knows all this. Whenever the critic returns, invite Love home with its essential reminders:

You are Love.

You are the one and only You.

You are worthy of every good thing.

THE CHOCOLATE CHIP COOKIE

Is there any food that says, "I love you!" like a perfect chocolate chip cookie? I don't think so.

Make these with your kids or for your kids. Give them to your friends and neighbors or, if you are like me, make them for yourself and prop a plate of those suckers on your chest while you binge Ted Lasso. But—always make these with love in your heart.

INGREDIENTS

Two sticks of softened butter (a half-pound)
1 1/4 cup brown sugar
1/2 cup white sugar
Two eggs
1 1/2 teaspoons vanilla
1 3/4 cups flour
1 teaspoon salt
1 teaspoon baking soda
1 1/2-2 cups chocolate chips

DIRECTIONS

Heat your oven to 375 degrees.

Beat your butter until fluffy and then add sugar.

Beat the butter and sugar together until smooth and creamy.

Add the eggs, while beating, one at a time.

Add vanilla.

In another bowl, add the flour, salt and baking soda.

Mix the dry and wet ingredients together and then stir in the chocolate chips.

Use a cookie scoop and bake on a parchment-lined cookie sheet for about eight minutes until golden brown.

Eat one. You heard me. Eat one while it's warm—one lovely bite at a time.

CHAPTER 6
O IS FOR OVER

I almost titled this chapter "Freedom."

I cannot say one pillar of FLOW is more significant than the others. But if I could, it would be this one.

Simply put, *you have a choice.*

Those words make my hair stand on end.

You have a choice in your thoughts.

In my coaching practice, one of two things happen when we get to the O section: people get very inspired or very triggered. I understand both reactions.

Learning we can choose our thoughts is scary. Admitting our thoughts are probably not true is scary. Learning we do not have to suffer at the hands of our thoughts is—freedom.

Freedom is scary.

The reality is that we are often addicted to our thoughts. We believe them, hook, line and sinker. Worse, we think they are us—if someone questions the credibility of our thoughts, it feels as if we are being attacked.

Say I have the thought that my neighbor is a jerk. We don't know what we don't know, so we fill in the blanks.

Here is the evidence: he is always yelling at his wife, he never says hello, and he never mows his lawn.

The evidence may point to him being a jerk, but knowing I have a choice, I choose to take a closer look and flip into curiosity.

Here are the things I didn't know: he is deaf, and he yells because he can't hear his volume; he grew up in WW2 Germany, and he doesn't trust people after seeing his parents taken to a concentration camp by neighbors; he has severe arthritis and lives on social security so he can't afford to care for the lawn to his or my standards. He is embarrassed about it, but there is nothing he can do.

Do you see where I am going?

Some people may be jerks, and some thoughts are true. The Over section is about questioning how much of your energy is used to carry around unproven thoughts that bring you down. Which set of thoughts above do you think would enable me to form a warm relationship with a kind and lonely neighbor? Which thoughts would make me more comfortable in my home, even if I never developed a relationship with Mr. Grumpypants? On the other hand, he could be a jerk. Without experiencing this person, we only have our thoughts and our internal stories to tell, and the path that brings us closest to flow is choosing Love.

Where do we start? As always, we go back to Finding. When we learn to observe those adorable little ping pong balls in our head that we call thoughts, we begin to understand the control we have over them. We can *choose* Love Over Worry.

It is perfectly normal to feel triggered at this point because if we accept that it is possible to control our thoughts, we now feel responsible. If I can choose my thoughts, then why do I feel so bad? Am I choosing to feel bad?

Unlikely.

Sometimes you might. You could be choosing the negative thought over the positive, Worry over Love. Other times you might be suffering from clinical depression, anxiety or a rash of crappy circumstances.

A word here on clinical depression. One of my clients has a daughter who suffered from clinical depression for many years, and she shared one of her survival techniques with me. When her daughter was depressed for more than a few days, unable to hold any positive thoughts, my client knew it was time to reach out for help. She knew that when nothing brought hope or release, her daughter was experiencing clinical depression and needed support.

I hope you will treat yourself with the same grace. If you can't find a reason for hope and nothing you usually love offers you relief, it's time to reach out for help. It may take a while to find it, and you may suffer in the meantime. But whatever you do, please keep reaching out and keep giving yourself grace.

If you are clinically depressed or have a severe anxiety disorder, trying to do this work could be challenging and even dangerous. You are not responsible for depression or any other brain health issue, and you deserve expert help and relief.

Your life circumstances may also be temporarily outside of your control. If you are in a moment or a cycle of challenging circumstances, your thoughts could be rolling in the mud more than usual. This is part of life. We are going to have hard times. The difference here is that you do have a choice about your thoughts! And there may be slight shifts that you can make in your circumstances once you shift your thoughts. When you are in a cycle of challenging circumstances but are not suffering from depression, you will find this work provides a respite. You'll have to work harder at it than you will when life is being sweet, but that work will pay off.

Using FLOW as my ongoing daily practice has greatly shifted my experiences in life. I am no longer chronically anxious, overwhelmed and ruminating. Dare I say I have changed? This practice worked for me, significantly changing my outlook on life. For that, I am deeply grateful.

Here is an example of the power of our thoughts. In this case, it starts with a TV show. I recently started watching *The Handmaid's Tale*, which should come with a warning: "May induce severe worry."

To be fair, I started watching while I was in mandatory two-week quarantine. I was isolated and tired and living through the third wave of a pandemic, primed to fall into a worry rabbit hole.

Just in case you've been camping in the Antarctic for the last five or so years, the show is a dystopian view of a future version of America. It is dark. Very dark. And the writer of the book on which it is based, Margaret Atwood, was extraordinary in her ability to predict a lot of the questions we're facing today. Ms. Atwood confessed in an interview that she did not put anything into the show that had not happened at some point in history. Putting it all together and turning a lens on these atrocities is jarring and terrifying.

I started to feel a heavy sense of foreboding. I had catastrophic thoughts about the future, getting lost in loops around everything from screen time to the environment. I was deep in a worry hole.

If I didn't understand how our brains work, I could so easily have stayed there. I could have begun to believe my distorted thinking. Instead, I noticed that I was having thoughts about the future that were not reality-based. It was one of those situations where there was absolutely no way to have enough information to draw credible conclusions. Worry is the nastiest form of fortune-telling, isn't it?

I had to take conscious timeouts to remember what was happening in my home and neighborhood, which was the usual status quo. No women wearing red capes were being hung in the town square. The world around me was moving as it always had. No one was shooting at my door or taking my kids away.

Yet, I had fallen into the fear created in a TV series. I had begun to believe the thought, "I am in danger." My mind had transformed these signals into a freeze-flee-fight state in my body's nervous system. Without my intervention, I would have been caught in a very grim feedback-response loop.

Our thoughts are this powerful. For many, the fear can draw us to more and more fear-based visuals and information. Worse, you don't even have to look—if you are online, algorithms will find you and send you sophisticated, micro-targeted propaganda that aligns with and intensifies your fear, whatever it may be.

Without intervention, these loops spiral until the brain hardwires to chronic paranoia and mistrust, the opposite of a flow state.

This awareness is especially vital for the times we live in. If we allow ourselves to get swept into a rabbit hole of negative news or even false information, we may not only believe it but may begin to behave as if it is real.

Our thoughts eventually become our actions. (More on this in the action chapter.) Our actions create our quality of life.

Positive or negative thoughts also determine our hormone levels, posture, facial expressions, tone of voice and energy levels. Our actions, and the state of our minds and bodies, have real-world consequences, good or bad.

Do we all agree it is wise to learn to manage our thoughts at this point? I thought so.

Do we all agree that it isn't easy? I thought so.

As you become accustomed to Finding, to observing your worry and unproven thoughts, you will catch yourself more and more often. Here is your masters-level practice insight: any discomfort you feel is a signal to scan your thoughts. Angry, embarrassed, frustrated, fearful—these are all clues that you might be in a worry loop with a lot of unproven thoughts.

When you see the thoughts, you can see the choice. If you choose to feel better, simply say to your thoughts, "I hear you. But I'm not convinced at this moment. Right now, I'm going to [take a walk, make those cookies, call a friend, take a bath?]. Why don't you get back to me when you have a lot more solid data?"

There is so much positive energy in just knowing we have a choice. When I started this work many years ago, although I was often swept away by my thoughts, I also started to feel a new sense of freedom. I knew that even when I was deep in a worry loop, there was a way out.

I started to become aware that I could feel better. I began to see I could take the driver's seat in my mind and my life.

Don't get me wrong. There were and are days when worry gets the best of me. When that happens, I go back to the beginning. I return to the 3M's. Then I start the Finding process. The difference between now and then is I am no longer afraid of getting stuck—I have a recipe to free myself from fear and worry-based thinking.

Choosing an alternative thought is like walking Over a bridge. On one side is the Worry thought. On the other side is Love.

Let's try it together right now.

Grab your notebook and write down a worry thought you had today.

Mine was: "I can't finish my work today because I don't have time."

Next, we need to observe the thought, to see it as a thought rather than a reality. We notice it and choose to walk Over the bridge to make a new, Love-based thought.

"I can finish my work today. I have enough time. I am grateful my husband is home—I can rely on him to handle the kids' needs."

Write your new thought, your Love thought, down in your notebook.

This power to choose a new thought will give you a sense of freedom and peace. Try it as often as you can when you notice a worry. It might feel intense at first because the beginning of learning anything involves the most heavy lifting—new things are hard until they are easy. Finding Love will get easy and will eventually be your default, your automatic go-to whenever you find yourself feeling uncomfortable.

Here is another example that does not involve a notebook.

I recently moved, again. I know! I should be writing a moving book at this point. Somewhere in the process, I had the inevitable thought, "How am I going to get this done!?"

I was overwhelmed and snapped at everyone. I was not sleeping well. Any time I caught the thought, I would stop, take a few deep breaths, and say to myself, "This will get done. You will find a way. You always find a way."

This Love thought gave me a sense of calm and the ability to think clearly and take the next steps.

I also sleep better when I use this recipe on those pesky thoughts that come up just as I'm about to drift off. FLOW can be very helpful with the nighttime woes, the moments when you are trying to fall into sleep and all you can think about are your myriad life challenges. When I am in the pre-sleep panic, I simply walk through the steps of FLOW. I notice each thought, and I replace it with something else. My "something else" is often, "I love this bed, and I love sleep!"

BITE-SIZE CAPRESE SALAD

This dish is one of my favorites to bring Over to a friend's house, especially for a summer barbecue or a casual hang on the porch. (Ha! See what I did there?)

This is so easy that I'm not sure it can even be called a recipe. Just add as much of each ingredient as you like or have on hand, and then add the dressing.

INGREDIENTS

Salad

Cucumber, cubed

Cherry tomatoes (halved)

Red onion (sliced thin)

Basil (chopped)

Avocado (cubed)

Pearl-sized mozzarella balls (or you can cube a mozzarella log)

Salt and pepper to taste

Optional: Corn cooked and then cut off the cob or diced roasted red peppers add to the deliciousness and make this more of a meal.

Dressing

3 tablespoons balsamic glaze or balsamic vinegar

1/2 cup olive oil

1-2 tablespoons agave (to taste)

Salt and pepper to taste

Optional: If you like a pop of spice, add a pinch of red pepper flakes.

DIRECTIONS

Mix all the salad ingredients in your favorite bowl.

Mix all the dressing ingredients in a jar and pour over the salad.

If possible, let everything come to room temperature before serving.

CHAPTER 7
W IS FOR WORRY

We've already talked a lot about Worry, but perhaps you are still resistant to the idea that it is something you can just walk away from. If you are convinced and have already put FLOW into practice, this chapter will be the icing on the cake.

According to the Merriam-Webster Dictionary, the definition of worry is to, "give way to anxiety or unease; allow one's mind to dwell on difficulty or troubles."

I'd like you to focus on those first two words, "give way." If we give way to something, we also have the choice not to give way. This is our choice.

Yes, it may seem impossible and overwhelming to resist giving way, but it is still our choice.

The next definition also implies a choice: "allow one's mind to dwell."

Do we allow our mind to dwell? Or direct our mind somewhere else?

As I've mentioned, my definition of worry is looped thoughts that cause unease and are based in fear and judgement rather than evidence.

Yes, we can believe these things are real.

Here's a tricky one: we can believe our intuition is telling us something through worry.

Intuition is like our emotions—it is there for us, and it is essential we pay attention to it. But intuition is a benevolent force. Even when it carries hard information, it still feels safe and calm. If you are about to step into an elevator with someone late at night and your intuition says you are unsafe, do not get into that elevator. However, if you have been in this situation, you will remember that intuition doesn't speak as worry. Intuition comes to us as a calm, aware kind of knowing. It slows down our thinking, while worry speeds up our thinking.

Worrying feels bad. It serves no purpose.

Let me say that again.

Worry serves no purpose.

In fact, challenge yourself right now to find a time when worry benefited you in some way. Can you? Most of us cannot. Worry steals our happiness and gives us nothing in return.

I cannot say this too often: worry is not in the same category as fear, anger, frustration, contempt, judgment, etc. It is not an emotion but a rumination. Emotions have benefits. Being in a flow state requires moving through our feelings rather than running from them or pushing them away. Bypassing our emotions by choosing replacement emotions and forcing happiness is nowhere in the FLOW recipe.

Something like fear can be very beneficial. Your house is on fire, and you do what you can to stay alive. Worrying about not finding a parking spot when you are running late? Not beneficial.

Trauma is often a precursor to worry, and chronic worry is a typical response to trauma. If you have experienced trauma and now experience chronic worry, I encourage you to reach out for help to continue your healing journey. I am a trauma survivor, and I have experienced both its disabling effects and the healing that is possible with compassionate trauma therapy[6].

I am also a recovering worrier. I've worried about the pipes bursting, lightning striking a tree near my house, my friends being mad at me, my car breaking down, the ache in my stomach being a tumor. You name it, I have worried about it.

I wasn't always a worrier. I was the girl who would jump out of an airplane or rock climb without ropes. My mom worried about my fearlessness. Then I had kids. Suddenly, I was afraid of my own shadow. My adrenal system was always in hyperdrive.

I tried many things to get my worry in check and didn't find anything that worked until I came up with FLOW. I still worry, much more than I would like, but now it is different. I know that my worries are not real. I have a technique to use when I begin to worry, and it works. FLOW works.

Remember myelin? The more you repeat a behavior, the more you will default to that behavior. The more you repeat thoughts, the more you will default to those thoughts.

[6] If personal trauma therapy isn't accessible for you right now, *How to Do the Work: Recognize Your Patterns, Heal from Your Past, and Create Your Self* by psychologist Nicole LaPera; *The Transformation, Discovering Wholeness and Healing After Trauma* by James S. Gordon, MD; and *The Body Keeps the Score: Brain, Mind and Body in the Healing of Trauma* by Bessel van der Kolk are all life-changing books on this subject.

If they are worry thoughts, then you will default to worry. If you practice the FLOW process, you will begin to default to flow. It is not fast. It is not easy. It is worth it. Feeling free is priceless.

ONE-BOWL CHOCOLATE ZUCCHINI CAKE

ONE-BOWL CHOCOLATE ZUCCHINI CAKE

Adapted from Mel's Kitchen Cafe

Why does chocolate make everything better?

Life is better when we enjoy the blessings of this Earth, like chocolate. I surely hope that all your worries will temporarily disappear when you sink your teeth into this cake.

Call it a miracle but this is the most requested birthday cake in our house. My mom made this to try to trick Miller into eating a vegetable and it became his favorite cake. I thought she was being a goofball and once again, she taught me a thing or two.

INGREDIENTS

3 large eggs
1 tablespoon vanilla extract
1 1/2 cups granulated sugar
3/4 cup buttermilk (Or substitute 3/4 cups regular or nut milk and 2 tablespoons lemon juice or vinegar; let sit for a few minutes before adding.)
1/2 cup melted coconut oil or unflavored vegetable oil like avocado, grape or canola
2 cups shredded zucchini
1 1/2 cups all-purpose flour
1/2 cup natural, unsweetened cocoa powder
1/2 teaspoon salt
1 teaspoon baking soda
1/4 teaspoon baking powder
For added richness or protein, add 3/4 cup small chocolate chips or chopped walnuts.

DIRECTIONS

Preheat your oven to 350 degrees F.

Lightly grease a 9”x13” pan, or 2, 8” round pans for a birthday cake, with cooking spray and set aside. (I always use aluminum or metal baking pans.)

In a large bowl, whisk together the eggs, vanilla, sugar, buttermilk and oil.

Stir in the shredded zucchini.

Add the flour, cocoa powder, salt, baking soda and baking powder.

Stir until no dry streaks remain.

Spread the batter evenly in the pan and bake for 25 to 35 minutes, until the top springs back lightly to the touch and a toothpick comes out clean or with a few moist crumbs.

Let cool completely.

Top with classic vanilla buttercream or whipped cream, or whatever your heart is longing for.

Here is my favorite vanilla buttercream frosting recipe:

INGREDIENTS

3 cups powdered sugar
1 cup softened butter
1 teaspoon vanilla
2-3 tablespoons whipping cream

DIRECTIONS

To your stand mixer bowl, add sugar and butter. Mix on low speed until it looks pale, white and fluffy, about 3 minutes. Add vanilla and cream and continue to beat on medium speed for about another minute, adding more cream if needed to reach spreading consistency.

CHAPTER 8
ACTION IT—YOUR MOMENT IN THE SPOTLIGHT

We are at an important turning point. Together, we have explored the 3M foundation and the four cornerstones of FLOW.

Now it is time to explore how this translates into a better life for you and yours.

Let's start with a 2020 study at Queens University in Canada[7], which found that we have more than six thousand thoughts each day!

Remember my story about Debbie, the nearsighted mom at my kids' school? If I was in the habit of believing my thoughts, I might have even stood up haughtily and moved to a different chair when I finally met her. I would have lost the opportunity to make a friend and to learn a valuable lesson. I would have continued thinking I was right about Debbie, and it might have reinforced other false stories I was telling myself.

Instead, good things happened in my life. I grew.

[7] Tseng, J., Poppenk, J. Brain meta-state transitions demarcate thoughts across task contexts exposing the mental noise of trait neuroticism. Nat Commun 11, 3480 (2020). https://doi.org/10.1038/s41467-020-17255-9

Now, multiply that by 6,000, and you'll get some idea of how much FLOW can improve the outcomes of our thoughts and actions and enrich our quality of life.

Let's examine a very common thought loop for women: weight. I don't know many women who do not think critically about the state of their bodies daily.

I will use myself as an example of the mental real estate taken up by intrusive worry thoughts. I have been self-conscious about my belly fat for as long as I can remember and I spend way too much time thinking about it. It has stopped me from wearing a two-piece bathing suit. It has even stopped me from being intimate with my husband because I was embarrassed by the way I looked. It has been a thought loop for many, many years, even though I exercise and eat well.

When we can see the time spent on any given loop, we can begin to build a strategy to confront it, a Love loop. In the case of my belly fat, I may use a strategy of acceptance, disrupting the worry loop with words of affirmation and gratitude for my body and my belly.

I might use a "get real" strategy: when I realize how much time I've spent shaming myself about my belly without it making a single fraction of an inch of a difference, it makes it easier to let go of the worry loop.

Another strategy might be following body acceptance advocates on social media—friends have told me that doing so has changed their lives. It's difficult to be happy when you hate part of yourself, and the sweetness that comes when you first look down and think, “Well, that’s normal!” is incomparable.

Whatever strategy I choose, I must first notice my thoughts. If I don’t, that is where my time and energy will go. Again, that’s the seductive thing about worry—it feels like we are doing something. But we are not. We are just in the loop.

Let’s grab the notebook again. Which worry loop will you challenge today? What’s your strategy? What is the action?

I’ve already given you one of mine, so I’ll use an example from another friend, Helen.

Helen explains her worry loop:

My friend Jan hasn’t called me in two weeks, and she usually calls once a week or more. Did I say something insensitive when we last talked? I feel like I was too heavy, ranting on and on about feeling overwhelmed.

Strategy:

Notice my feelings and thoughts and realize they are telling me how much I value Jan. Notice the importance Jan has in my life. Get curious and check in with her about my concern. Be transparent and open.

Actions:

Text Jan to tell her I’m thinking about and missing her. Ask if she’s up for a call and decide that I’ll drop over and check to make sure she’s okay if I haven’t heard back from her by the end of the day. Plan to make a point of expressing appreciation for our friendship when next we speak.

In this example, you can feel the empowerment that comes from observing and strategizing. Also, this allows Helen to move on from her worry story. Regardless of the outcome, she now has a plan. The brain space that was obsessing about whether she'd offended Jan is now free to consider new possibilities.

Even the energy around their friendship will change. Instead of nonverbally communicating distress, Helen will radiate Love and gratitude.

REFRIGERATOR PASTA

This simple recipe feels right for the action chapter because most of our refrigerators need to be cleaned out. I like to avoid this tedious task, but the day finally comes that I take action and I feel so much better when I do.

For this recipe, you need a few baseline ingredients, and the rest can come from the back and bottom of your fridge.

INGREDIENTS

Olive oil
Garlic
Salt and pepper
Whatever veggies you have in the fridge that may be past their best but are still okay to eat. Broccoli, zucchini, cauliflower, peppers, mushrooms ... anything that is still edible.
Herbs and spices that you love. I am a fan of tarragon, oregano and red pepper flakes. Maybe a pinch of white pepper. You choose!

DIRECTIONS

Chop your veggies into roughly equal chunks.

Toss with olive oil, salt and pepper.

Roast for about 15 minutes at 425 degrees.

Heat your pasta water, and when it's at a rolling boil, add as many servings as you need. (I like linguine for this.) Set your timer.

While your vegetables are roasting, heat a few tablespoons of olive oil to low-medium in a large skillet and sauté the garlic.

When the veggies are roasted, add them to the skillet.

This is where you can get creative. Add red pepper flakes, oregano, thyme or nothing. Top with parmesan, feta or even mozzarella. (One of my aspiring vegan friends adds nutritional yeast mixed with toasted panko breadcrumbs and a bit of salt.)

When the pasta is done, take 1/3 cup of the starchy water from the pot and add it to the skillet for extra creaminess.

Drain and toss the pasta into the skillet.

Stir everything together.

Put it in a bowl and enjoy it with a piece of that bread you made earlier!

CHAPTER 9
THE GREAT DISTRACTIONS

Sex, money, power, screens, drugs, work, food—what's your poison?

This chapter is about all the things that may keep you from your FLOW journey.

Let's talk about those pesky (and sexy) distractions, the things that will seduce and tempt you away from your spiritual growth. I use the word "seduce" because, man, are they fun! Many are so highly valued in Western societies that it can be nearly impossible to discern what is truly praiseworthy and what is an ego- or escape-driven distraction.

It's a good time to add a disclaimer of sorts. I'm not suggesting distractions are bad!! Many of the things that end up in this column add great flavor to life. Only when they keep us from our growth and awakening are they troublesome.

For instance, let's say you have had your heart broken. You are devastated; you cry at every toilet paper commercial. Well, most commercials.

This is a natural and beautiful time in a life. It is certainly painful, but this is the good kind of pain—pain that can result in deep awareness and growth if we allow it. If, after four or five days, you still reach for the remote control, or the wine or a revenge hook-up each time you feel like you can't bear the hurt, you can be sure the great distractions are holding you back. They are getting between you and your evolution. And here's the real bummer: if you bypass this growth moment, you may feel better, but the lesson will come again and again, often with more intensity (and more pain) than on the first pass.

The lessons we are meant to learn will find their way to us. I believe that because I've seen it so often in my own life and the lives of others. They often come at us with a soft nudge first, but they quickly escalate into a solid slap when we refuse to listen. Understanding this can help us avoid great suffering by learning the lesson the first time, by not distracting ourselves from the awakening.

To equip you with even more awareness for the hard times, let's talk about what I think of as the "Four Major Distractions," sex, money, power and drugs.

Sex: I am not just talking about the horizontal tango, but about anything related to sexuality that occupies your thoughts and makes you feel "high." Sexual attraction or allure can be an addiction when used to avoid discomfort. When I moved to New York City in my twenties, I could barely think about anything other than boys! I wasn't having sex, but I was obsessed with dating, my appearance and flirting. I'd just left an abusive relationship, and I decided to be abstinent but date as much as possible, a plan I thought would protect my wounded heart.

My strategy worked in that I didn't get emotionally attached to the men I was dating. But I was fully obsessed with my dating life and the distraction kept me from feeling the hurt left over from my volatile relationship. Don't get me wrong—I was having the time of my life. I almost want to write a book about that year because it was right out of a "Sex in The City" episode (without the sex). Manolo Blahniks knock-offs and a bevy of men were my daily bread.

Until I had to pay the piper. When a true, real relationship came into my life, I was initially able to distract, distract, distract. But once I started to fall in love, I had to deal with my fear and insecurities from my past relationship. Luckily, I fell in love with a man who could walk with me through my healing. The story could have had a much different ending if I'd chosen distraction over my growth once again. Like I said, your lessons will eventually find you, no matter what.

Drugs: This category can include, but is not limited to, alcohol, illicit or prescription drugs, sugar, food and screens. Digital distractions might have even surpassed actual drugs in this category. Devices are our current "crack epidemic."

We have all become reliant on digital accessories to one degree or another. I recently visited a friend whose entire house is run by her phone. Lights turn on and off, doors open and close, the temperature is managed—even the coffee can be made by pushing the right buttons on her smartphone. It was amazing and unnerving. Every time she needed to do something in her home, she had to pick up her phone. Every time she picked up her phone, there was an unread text or an alert to check Twitter, or an email had come in from a potential client.

Just opening the blinds can now be interrupted by a litany of new information and demands on her time. The boundaries between the needs of the outside world and her needs have been breached.

Do you use your phone as your alarm clock? Then you will understand this conundrum. I often tell my kids that there will never be anything more exciting and enticing than their screens. I have heard stories of kids rejecting Disney World in favor of free time to play Fortnite. My household could fall right into this dynamic if it weren't for my tenacity and awareness of where this all leads.

Do I sound like my mother, with her disdain for TV in the nineties? I can still hear her: "That thing is going to melt your brain!" In retrospect, my parents were right to be wary of the television consumption in our home. To this day, I turn to the TV as my drug of choice. When I am exhausted or overwhelmed, emotionally drained or angry, I sit down with a box of cookies and the remote.

Money, Power and Overwork: Then there is that almighty dollar and its clingy cousin overwork. We live in a society in which chasing money and power is praised and admired. It can be a sweet part of life until their pursuit becomes the driving force in our life and our personal and spiritual growth is neglected.

A good example of money as a distractor comes in the form of a moral question. It's one I am faced with often when I am asked to work with brands. It can be tough to turn down large sums of money when products or companies do not align with my values. I like to believe that I have been true to my moral compass, but I can see how easy it would be to rationalize and take the cash. Over time, it's possible to compromise our values too many times and lose ourselves. I mean, I don't have to tell you—you've watched "Breaking Bad," right?

However, if you have bypassed your values to put food on the table at some point, that is okay. Sometimes we must survive by any means necessary, and there is no shame in that. None. Shaming ourselves usually ends with reaching for more great distractions. Instead, notice what you are feeling (Finding), then consciously choose to cross Over that bridge to Love.

It's a process. Wake up each day and use the FLOW recipe to identify any pleasures that have become distractions from your authentic power and spiritual path.

Notice which distractions you reach for when you are uncomfortable. The great social scientist Dr. Brené Brown has spoken about feeling like she needed many 12-step programs when she first got sober because she was a "take-the-edge-off-aholic."

Do you have one or many distractions of choice? In addition to my cookie and TV habit, I used drugs and alcohol for most of my adult life to avoid feeling. I wasn't blacking out, but I was choosing a glass of wine over a tough conversation or taking a Xanax to fall asleep when my mind was swirling. I still sometimes do. The difference today is that I make room for a beat between feeling my feelings and pouring any wine. I now take the time to check in with myself about what is going on. I walk myself through FLOW and see how I feel on the other side.

If I choose to have the wine because I don't want to feel, I know those feelings will come back to knock on my door soon. I may decide that's okay. But it is more likely I'll forgo the wine this time and let the feelings wash over and through me.

The key is consciousness. I don't know about you, but I am not looking for a life without screens, wine, cheese, sex or money. I just want to be fully conscious when I am engaging with those beautiful gifts!

KNOW YOUR TRIGGERS

When are you most likely to fall into the distraction bucket? My trigger is exhaustion. I have a clear pattern: I push and push, and then I completely shut down. When I shut down, I watch TV, eat cookies, take sleep aids, etc.

Once I see the pattern, though, I can plan to avoid the otherwise inevitable dive into the cookie dough. In this example, I now allow myself to admit when I am pushing myself past my body's ability. I may be saying yes when I mean no. I may offer up my time when I know I am too busy or too tired. Once I can see the issue, I can change the pattern.

We are taught to start with, "Don't eat a box of cookies in front of the TV." We know how that turns out, right? Shame and sorrow. Instead, let's learn to start with, "Listen to our bodies and our feelings."

We want to treat the cause, not the symptom.

As I write these words, I am keenly aware of what a challenge it is to be fully conscious of the way we're engaging with distractions. Like I said, they are sexy! And they aren't the bad guy.

The key is to see where you are being pulled from your highest vibration, your authentic self, your spiritual path. Then it is time to get to work.

Here's a bit of good news: once we are conscious, we can engage in the big distractions with awareness and intentionality.

If we aren't using *Game of Thrones* to avoid our feelings, we can enjoy it for the magic that it is. And if I'm planning a cookie binge, I can make the great ones from Chapter 5 instead of reaching for the boxed kind. Win/win!!

JESSICA'S BAKED BRIE

JESSICA'S BAKED BRIE

Okay, kids, this one is so naughty it seemed perfect for the distractions chapter.

My sister-in-law turned me on to this a few years ago, and I feel like I am having an elicit cheese affair when I make it. It is straight-up scandalous!

INGREDIENTS

One brie round
3 tablespoons butter
Brown sugar
Sliced almonds
Sliced apple
Baguette

DIRECTIONS

Preheat your oven to 350 F.

Put the brie in an oven-safe dish.

Cut the butter into slices and place it on top of the cheese. (I know, I know.)

Top the butter with packed brown sugar.

Top the sugar with sliced almonds.

Bake for about 20 minutes.

Serve with a thinly sliced baguette and sliced apples.

Don't be mad at me. This will be a problem, but isn't it a good problem?

CHAPTER 10

YOUR HYPNOTIST & MY ENGLISH BREAKFAST

We've been here before—about to face down a simultaneously triggering and liberating idea. The trigger is being challenged to give up the comforts of believing we cannot control our mindset. The liberation comes from the truth that we can!

"Be aware of your hypnotist" is a little less intense than "Beware your hypnotist!" but go with whatever works in your life right now. If you need to have a serious detox, then go directly to "beware." If you are just a little uncomfortable with the thoughts in your head, "be aware." Either way, just know this is important.

Okay, what am I talking about? I am talking about anything that influences you. It might be social media, television, a workshop, a class, a song, a friend, your family—the list is endless.

We are hypnotized by any stimuli we take in, which can be a good and very pleasurable experience. Think about being at a concert by your favorite artist. You will be mesmerized. Hypnotized.

Imagine watching *Schitt's Creek* or any show you are currently binging. Hours pass, and you still haven't eaten— unless you are me and you have mindlessly eaten a whole box of cookies. But I digress.

What podcasts do you listen to when you walk? (Hopefully, FLOW.) What playlist do you have on while you clean? What workshop or class did you sign up for recently?

Here is where it gets tricky. Some of these things fall in the category of helpful and mind-expanding (FLOW—wink, wink). But what if the song you are listening to is Rage Against the Machine talking about "F you, I won't do what you tell me"? You may be getting your groove on, but you are also subconsciously absorbing a concept. In this case, to ignore everyone and angrily do whatever you want to do.

I love music, even Rage Against the Machine, and I love that song when I work out and need adrenaline. All of that is A-okay—if you are aware of the influence these lyrics and others have on you.

One frightening example of this phenomena at work right now is the number of young women asking plastic surgeons to make them look like social media filters.

If our brains have not caught on to this almost constant hypnotism, we will base real decisions with real consequences on unexamined inputs. If you listen to self-help podcasts and read self-help books, then that is what you will think about most of the time. The same goes for any category. It can be beneficial if you are a cardiac surgeon and all you read and listen to are books on the heart. Your brain is then hyper-focused and hardwired to understand the complexities of heart surgery. We would categorize this as a good thing.

How about when your inputs are all from a so-called self-help group that ends up being a cult, like my friend Sarah Edmondson? Part of the cult's process was to completely immerse the participants in its world. They became hypnotized to the degree that they agreed to be physically branded and controlled by the cult's leader, Keith Raniere.

Sarah's is an extreme example, but for a more everyday one, let's go back to my intense experience with *The Handmaid's Tale* and quarantine. Only my FLOW practice saved me from what could have been a painful, destructive downward emotional spiral.

When we embark on any journey, especially a spiritual one, we must be aware that we are being influenced. I am influencing you at this very moment. See how tricky this is?

The best way to maintain your awareness and guard against total immersion is to regularly turn off all inputs and take time for quiet and meditation, or even just a walk. (Yes, we are back to the 3M's.)

Disconnecting recalibrates your brain to your own guiding lights.

Here is another metaphor, one I use often to help my clients wrap their heads around this concept.

When I first moved to England at sixteen, we stayed in a bed and breakfast on the first night. In the morning, I went to the breakfast room and was served a classic English breakfast. My plate included eggs, bacon, toast, black pudding, baked beans, roasted tomatoes and mushrooms. I was flummoxed, to say the least. I had never seen a breakfast like it. Obviously, I ate it, and I loved it, but it was new and confusing to me. Was this supposed to be my whole day's food on one plate? Did this happen every day? And what in the world is black pudding?

Have breakfast in Japan if you want to get this on an even deeper level! A traditional Japanese breakfast consists of steamed rice, miso soup, a protein such as grilled fish, and various side dishes, usually fermented vegetables.

Definitely not your typical American breakfast of eggs and bacon, pancakes or cereal.

My point is this: our mindset is a product of the world around us. The culture around us, the rituals around us. Until we encounter something new, we can believe our culture is the only way to live. But what if you never encounter something new? What if you just stay conditioned to the ways of the world you are accustomed to, to the ways you have been influenced?

There is incredible nuance in the world. And there are so many ways we are hypnotized every single day.

I have recently been consuming an Instagram feature called Reels. These are ten- to fifteen-second videos. When one finishes, it automatically scrolls to the next. It is very easy to spend two hours with these bite-size videos and come out wondering what just happened to your day. I do not know why the algorithm decided I love DIY home projects, but that seems to be the lion's share of the videos I see. Don't get me wrong—I love a cute bathroom remodel. It just isn't a passion for me. Yet, after losing myself in these videos, I noticed I was feeling unhappy with my current bathroom. Which is quite lovely, by the way. Which does not need an upgrade. But if I were not dedicated to FLOW and being aware of what my thoughts are up to, I'd be calling around for a good contractor.

Be discerning. Enjoy it all with your eyes wide open.

We are living in the age of information. You can learn just about any skill by searching online. The world is truly at your fingertips. That is exciting and empowering until it becomes a replacement for your intuition, reflection and values.

It is paramount we make pockets of time to protect our minds from all external input. Your intuition is your guide to your life purpose—if you can't hear it because of the cacophony pumping from the many external sources in your life, you may miss the boat.

Take some time each day to notice what influences you. Then take some time to check in on you. Are your influences in alignment with your values and the life you're building?

Shall we grab the notebook?

What media did you consume today?

How did it make you feel?

How much time was spent taking in information today?

How did it make you feel?

How much time did you spend in quiet?

How did it feel?

You get the picture. Keep going.

WHIPPED FETA

I first tried this intoxicating combination at a restaurant in Florida —sweet, salty and utterly sinful.

Everyone at the table fell silent when they took the first bite. You could make people cluck like chickens for more if you wanted to with this hypnotizing recipe.

INGREDIENTS

8 ounces feta
1/2 cup plain Greek yogurt (you could use sour cream for even more richness)
1 clove garlic
1 teaspoon fresh rosemary or thyme or both, minced
Honey
Marcona almonds
Warm pita or naan

DIRECTIONS

Put the first 4 ingredients in a food processor and blend. If it is too thick, add a little olive oil, milk or cream. Don't add any salt until you taste it because feta can be so salty.

Put the whipped feta in a bowl and drizzle with warm honey. Sprinkle Marcona almonds on the top and around the bowl. Serve with warm pita triangles.

CHAPTER 11

YOU WILL NEVER BE FULLY SATISFIED. STOP TRYING TO BE.

The most common discomfort my clients reveal in our initial meetings is the sense that they aren't where they are supposed to be. Further, they don't have the time, ability, resources, etc., to get there.

In their words, they are deeply dissatisfied most of the time. Even when they are on vacation, they start thinking about the complexities of the journey home and work that is waiting. Some start planning the next vacation when they are on vacation.

Here's the thing.

Our minds are wired to be dissatisfied. It was a valuable survival advantage until a few generations ago. Those who were always striving for more were more likely to survive famines and wars, creating an evolutionary advantage. We are hardwired to seek constantly, which means we are hardwired to miss the goodness right in front of us.

A friend called me today and told me that, after forty years of striving, waking up every day with the heavy feeling she was behind and would never catch up, she woke up this morning and thought, "What a beautiful to-do list I have today."

The difference between those two thoughts is the difference between happiness and unhappiness for her, she said—the difference between living in peace and living life in chronic stress and shame.

How did she do it? It was an accident. She is the editor of this book, and she put the FLOW recipe to work in her life to test whether this written direction translates effectively into real-life application.

It started working under the surface of her consciousness, and she woke up Over the Love bridge.

Lori is committed to constant personal growth, and she is also extremely practical. She is savvy when it comes to this type of content and has read and edited countless books in this genre. I love to work with her because I know she will call out any shenanigans. She's spent more than thirty years growing and healing from trauma by reading self-help books, yoga and meditation practice, therapy, twelve-step programs and Buddhism. So, when she told me that FLOW was the tool that created this life-changing shift for her, I cried. I know it sounds dramatic, but I cried, in solidarity as well as gratitude. We deserve to feel good. Lori said it was the "bite-size" nature of FLOW that made the difference in her breakthrough—it was easy to keep it with her as she moved through the busiest days, unlike other practices that seemed to pile up on her to-do list. Once she went Over to a Love thought, her other practices, like yoga and meditation, felt accessible again.

Mary Oliver wrote, so beautifully, "Tell me what it is you plan to do. With your one wild and precious life."

Well, Lori and I? We will FLOW. Join us?

When Oprah finishes an interview, she often asks, "What do you know for sure?"

I have played out the way I would answer this question if I were ever asked. (By Oprah, of course.)

Obviously, I would first go blank, because don't we always think of the best answer after the fact?

Because I am writing this book, though, I have been able to think a lot about my answer. It is: "We never suffer in the present moment."

It is hard to stay in touch with the present moment, isn't it? We often cast our minds into the future (worry and anxiety) or the past (shame, sadness, regret and comparison). Then we will do almost anything to avoid feeling the way those thoughts make us feel. (See the Great Distractions chapter.)

Gratitude is so transformative partly because it brings us back into the present moment. For as long as we stay there, we are at peace. Even the most difficult emotions can flow through us, but as the Buddhists say of this state, "We are the sky, and our emotions are the weather."

Lori told me another story, a beautiful illustration of the value of this practice. Twenty or so years ago, a friend of hers lost her twenty-year-old son. Family and friends gathered, and Lori was among them. On one of these days, as stories of this beautiful young man's life were shared, his mom collapsed, sobbing helplessly into her lap, her back bent by anguish. Everyone in the room could feel her pain. It was physical and almost unbearable. Her brother moved over to sit beside her and rub her back. Some time passed, and another story was told, and then another. She sat up again, quietly. By the end of the story, she was laughing helplessly, wiping tears from her eyes and holding her sides. Everyone in the room was.

Lori set a new life goal for herself: to develop such strength, openness and awareness that she could face her own life tragedies with similar grace, moving from disabling grief to helpless laughter by staying present to the moments that arise. To be wide open to being human and to life.

This presence is what I mean when I say, "We can never suffer in the moment." There are exceptions, yes—but they are fleeting if we are willing to let them go, even when the pain is the most unbearable suffering humans know, like losing a child.

Sometimes, dissatisfaction or self-induced suffering comes to us in the form of nostalgia.

Merriam-Webster's definition of nostalgia is, "a sentimental longing or wistful affection for the past, typically for a period or place with happy personal associations."

Nostalgia happens to be one of my favorite drugs. It is the ultimate temptress, so seductive while seeming so harmless. We use tools to evoke nostalgia, such as music and smells. When you are with friends or family, notice how often the conversation goes to past experiences. It may be in the form of re-telling a childhood antic; your friend may wax poetic about her college conquests.

These are fun, aren't they? Rolling around in all that sugar-coated history.

Recently we've had a brutal heat wave in our area. The temperature broke records, topping 117 degrees. It was hot. Very hot. My kids were grumpy and uncomfortable, so I decided to take notes from my childhood. Cold towels for everyone. I opened all the windows, hanging sheets on the south-facing ones to deflect the heat of the sun. I made a big pitcher of lemonade and bought the kids some popsicles. My body was zapped of energy, so I decided to take a day off. I pulled out an antique fan that was shockingly efficient and sat in my room to read. The house was quiet; even the birds seemed silenced by the heat. I could smell the sea and feel the stickiness of my skin.

As I gazed out my window, I was transported to an island called Tortola. Down to the hum of the old fan, my bedroom felt like the house where I stayed there. It wasn't long before my mind was fully immersed in that time. I was in my early twenties, dating a man I thought I loved. I remembered the freedom I felt. I reveled in my gorgeous, toned body. I remembered the fresh mango tree that stood outside the bedroom window, close enough I could reach out and pluck its luscious fruit.

I chose to stay in this memory for a few minutes. I even began to pine for that feeling.

This is nostalgia.

What nostalgia leaves out is the truth. Wasn't it sexy and fun? Nope. I was in an abusive relationship. I was broke because we spent all our money on trips we could not afford. And, frankly, I was often annoyed. I was surrounded by strapping men surfing, but I usually sat on the beach as a spectator. I denied my passions to make room for those of my boyfriend[8].

Now, before we go down the path of people-pleasing (the next chapter), I want to shine a light on the dark side of nostalgia. Nostalgia's job is to convince you that a filtered version of your past was the best part of your life. Lies!!!

Unless we unpack the many sides of these nostalgic memories, we can easily stay locked in this rose-colored vision of past perfection.

To avoid living in dissatisfaction, we must stay fully conscious of any desire to live somewhere else. That's true especially when the "somewhere else" is in our past.

That day in the heatwave, when I came back to the present, I saw the abundance of my life. My healthy relationship. My soft body, which miraculously carried those three humans playing outside. The cherry tree outside extending its branches toward me. I saw the magic.

Now, you might find yourself traveling into nostalgia that doesn't have a dark underbelly. For instance, I recently was transported to a moment in my childhood when a family friend taught me to make homemade, from-scratch hot chocolate. I could smell the room, hear her voice and taste the warm chocolate. I was nostalgic for the pure simplicity of that time.

I began to wish my kids had family and family friends nearby. I began to wish for something I did not have. I began to feel scarcity and lack. There was no negative inside of this memory.

[8] This was not his fault. I was a product of my culture and upbringing, conditioned to put others' needs before my own.

It was beautiful and pure, which is why I mention it here. This kind of nostalgia is a guidepost. If you often travel to another time in your mind and that time was healthy, it is a useful breadcrumb trail, a guide toward a desire you may not have known you had.

What about your memory is pleasing to you? What did you feel? What makes you feel this way in the present?

Even if you cannot think of anything that replicates this feeling and that you can engage in more, you have a new guidepost toward your passion.

In my hot chocolate memory, I mostly felt safe. That is the feeling. I asked myself what makes me feel safe right now. How can I expand that experience?

The answer was family dinner. Is that not amazing? My spirit immediately answered my question. I can devote more energy to family dinner, growing the sense of safety that my nostalgia brought to my attention.

Try this on your nostalgia favorites.

HOMEMADE HOT CHOCOLATE WITH WHIPPED CREAM

INGREDIENTS

4 cups whole milk
1/4 cup unsweetened cocoa powder
1/4 cup granulated sugar
1/2 cup chocolate chips
1/4 teaspoon vanilla
pinch of salt
2 cups heavy whipping cream
2 teaspoons sugar
1/4 teaspoon vanilla extract

DIRECTIONS

In a small saucepan, heat milk, sugar and cocoa powder. Don't let it boil. When it is hot, add the chocolate chips. Whisk until everything is melted and combined, then whisk in the vanilla extract. Sprinkle with a pinch of salt and put aside while you whip the cream.

Whisk the cream, sugar and remaining vanilla together, by hand if you want an arm workout. Or, put this in a standing mixer with your whisk attachment and whisk until you get firm peaks.

Pour the hot chocolate into mugs and top with whipped cream. You can sprinkle with cinnamon or simply enjoy as is!

CHAPTER 12

PEOPLE-PLEASING, THE ANTI-FLOW

I was sitting in my therapist's office, exhausted and resentful, recounting the struggles of my week and how depleted I was feeling.

He calmly listened to me. Gently, he said, "Kelley, you are a people-pleaser. You suffer from codependent patterns that are left over from childhood trauma. I suggest you start going to meetings for codependence. I really think it would help you."

Say what?

Was he talking to me? I simply love people. I want to help when I can. I am a good friend. I am a good wife. My list went on and on.

It has taken me years of therapy to see the damaging addiction I had to people-pleasing and the devastating effects it had on my health. I saw it as black and white: if I don't help people, then I am selfish. I had been a people-pleaser for so long that when my therapist asked me simple questions such as, "How do *you* feel?" I often could not answer.

Pleasing people is as familiar to me as breathing oxygen. When I finally began to accept my people-pleasing diagnosis, I was scared and overwhelmed.

Then I was invigorated and determined to shift this pattern of mine.

Here are some classic signs you are a people-pleaser, paraphrased from *Psychology Today*:

1. You're upset if everyone doesn't like you.
2. You apologize a lot, often for no good reason.
3. You are hungry for validation.
4. People ask you for too much.
5. Boundaries? What are they?
6. You hate conflict.
7. You follow the rules.
8. You think self-care is a nice luxury.
9. You are anxious.
10. You judge yourself by the highest standards.
11. You don't know how to ask for what you want or need.
12. You're sensitive to criticism.
13. You consider your feelings, needs, opinions and ideas less important than other people's.
14. You're attracted to people who need you, and you try to solve their problems.
15. You sometimes resent the people you love and feel they should try harder to understand your feelings and needs.

I feel a little like a soldier standing on the battlefield while the cannons are still smoking, taking in the damage, still stoked with adrenaline. I am not the wise sage who looks back at that battlefield with years of clarity. I am the fighter who is done with the fight but who barely yet understands its wreckage.

I do not identify with all the qualities of a classic people-pleaser. I do not shy away from conflict, although I don't make it. I do not expect myself to be perfect, and I do not undervalue my ideas. My version of people-pleasing comes in the form of caretaking. I have been a chronic caretaker.

There was a time in my life when I thought it was my best quality. I felt my ability to "read your mind" and fulfill your needs was a superpower. I thought I was helping.

What I didn't know was that my "superpower" was also my kryptonite. It was slowly killing me. I now see my chronic caretaking like this: I was the drug dealer. I had the goods, and I would get you hooked. I was looking for addicts so I would never be alone; they would need me. Whenever I took my drug away, they felt rejected, hurt and often eventually angry.

I now understand that many of my relationships were built on this cracked foundation. I am rewriting many of my relationships, and I vow to never again pull out that bag of caretaking crack. This commitment does not mean I can't take care of people I love, but that I must do so with full consciousness. (See the chapter on Finding.)

When I reflect on how someone might feel in response to my caretaking, I see this twisted dynamic with total clarity. Who wouldn't want to have their favorite meals waiting, gifts on their bed, all-expenses-paid outings planned and an endless ear for compassionate listening? I mean, I want that drug. That's the twisted part—we all want that drug. Being seen, even when it comes from an unhealthy place, is so luxurious. We are so deprived of the true presence of others that we will take focused attention from the most depleted source to feel that elusive feeling. That is why I never wanted for more souls to show up on my doorstep.

My husband tried to intervene many times, asking me why I was "killing myself" to make someone else's experience extraordinary. I neglected my work, my health and even my kids.

Most people cannot see their part in these complex relationships. They are too busy reveling in the glow to notice that what they're receiving is too much. In my case, even if someone had pushed back, I don't think I would have listened. I was a machine. A people-pleasing machine.

When I was a young girl, I was acutely aware that my role was service. I remember spending hours cleaning the house before my mom got home from work. I even had dinner ready and I didn't forget to dust the baseboards. I was ten years old. My parents had not asked for this duty—I intuitively tuned into the needs of my family, and I loved the look of relief on their faces when they walked through the door.

I don't remember why I felt compelled to over-serve back then. But being a mom, going to therapy and getting certificates and degrees in psychology and coaching has helped me understand.

I was lonely. Deeply lonely. When I served others, I received praise and attention. Maybe those dinners forced everyone to fawn over me and compliment my work. It made me feel that I was valued and needed.

Being a mom myself, I can see how my mother loved my help. She was tired. She worked full time, and she and my father had recently reconciled after a five-year separation—I'm guessing her life was complex and challenging. We did not live near our extended family and my childhood was isolated and quiet.

I was loved. That I do not doubt. But I was not the center of anyone's life, and so I made myself needed to fill that emptiness.

There is a method used in psychology that involves slowly approaching your childhood home in your mind. Eyes closed, breathing deeply. Put your hands over your heart and look through the window until you find yourself as a child.

What do you see? How do you feel? How is the little you feeling?

When I do this exercise, I see that I felt lonely. Unsure.

My father is an acclaimed archeologist, and I've heard him teach about early cultures. A cornerstone of their survival was community. We would not be here if it weren't for community. People who left or were pushed from their tribes didn't often survive for long.

When extended families began to splinter geographically, something happened. I'm the product of this shift in evolution. I grew up as a child of the generation that began to regularly move away from their families of origin. If you are reading this book, you probably are as well.

I learned to survive by making myself needed. My empathic heart was the exact tool I needed to become the best dealer on the block.

Until I wasn't.

For me, waking up was a slow process. I was revered for my caretaking abilities. I'll never forget when a friend came to visit me at our home in Park City, Utah. We had babies only a few months apart, and when she came for a visit, they were both two-year-olds. Busy and barely napping two-year-olds.

I spent weeks preparing for their visit, making sure to have all their favorite snacks, reservations at family-friendly outings, meals prepped and planned. (I even left out gluten because of their new diet.) I turned down the beds at night, turned on the ocean sounds for the baby and set out a glass of wine for my friend when she came up from the bath I ran for her. I also paid for everything. No one asked me to, and they often tried to stop me.

There was no stopping me. I was an addict of the highest order. Addicted to people-pleasing.

One morning, I woke early to put the homemade cinnamon rolls in the oven. Are you getting uncomfortable yet with the grotesque level of caretaking you are reading about? I am. My friend's toddler was awake, so I was juggling breakfast and the kids. The clock continued to tick forward until it was time to make lunch, with no sign of my friend.

Where were they? She and her husband were still sleeping, and it was now noon.

I tried to keep the kids quiet and occupied, but rage began to build slowly within me. It was the first time in my adult life that I took a thirty-thousand-foot view of what was happening. As my anger grew, I finally decided to knock on the door.

"What is going on? It is one o'clock! Your son has been crying for you for hours."

My friend said, "I thought you had him. Why are you so mad? You love this!"

You. Love. This.

Those three words still sting my heart. I love this? I love being a nanny, cook, housekeeper and bank account for everyone? Do I love this? HELL NO!

I was so angry that it took me a moment to understand her confusion. She had only known me to be an endless faucet of caretaking. Why would I rebel? Isn't this how it worked?

None of this was her fault.

I have come to understand that we must believe that caretaking at this level equals love at this level. It feels too good to question. We are all so deprived of deep love and attention that no one wants to turn off the faucet, including the faucet.

It is a widespread disorder in our culture and, until we all see the pattern, we are destined to pass it onto our kids (especially our girls).

Those of you with kids will understand this awakening. Especially those of you with kids and mothers who are not caretakers—we often mother our mothers as well as our children. I also think many of the grandmothers I see devoting their blood, sweat and tears to their children and grandchildren are just like I was, without the grace of an awakening.

Let me be clear. Giving of yourself is a beautiful thing and being of service to others is the pinnacle of any spiritual journey. The difference between being of service and people-pleasing is in the reasons behind your actions. When we are people-pleasing, we are looking to fill a void. When we are of service, we pour from a full cup—we don't need validation or even gratitude. We serve for ourselves as well as others, and we draw boundaries that allow us to do so sustainably and in good health.

People-pleasing is when your service is rooted in fear. Fear of being left. Fear of being alone. Fear of not being loved.

The FLOW journey can bring us to a place where service pours from a cup that never empties because it is constantly refilled by our self-worth and self-love, and protected by firm boundaries.

In a FLOW world, your worth is no longer connected to the needs and approval of those around you. Instead, it is steadily and thoughtfully replenished by you, every day. Then and only then can you offer your service to another in a way that fills your spirit and theirs.

It may take time to undo a lifetime of people-pleasing, so remember to start small. I started by waking up a little earlier than my family. It was enough time to enjoy a coffee, read a passage in my book or get a little meditation in. That small act of self-love gave me more space to serve the people I love.

I have now made that morning time non-negotiable. Anytime I think I can't, I pretend that I am catching a flight. (I will never miss a flight!) When I apply the same determination to my morning routine, I rarely miss it.

I have also adopted a quick technique I call the FLOW Countdown for whenever someone asks me to do something or I feel compelled to offer my services.

Finding—Does this feel good?

Love—Would I *love* to help? Not just be okay with, but find meaning or joy in?

Over—Do they have another option aside from my help?

Worry—Will this make me feel resentful or stressed?

I can quickly ask myself these questions before I engage or commit. If the answers lead me to a yes, I raise my hand or throw my hat in the ring. If they lead me to a no, I decline and offer my compassion but not my time.

Boundaries are essential in breaking codependent patterns. "Boundaries" can seem like one of those "self-love" words, often used and rarely explained. Another friend told me about going to Google and asking, "What is an emotional boundary?" before reading some basic information and realizing, "Oh, yeah. I don't have any of those."

You will have a much more attuned internal compass when you have used the FLOW recipe for a while. This work will help you see the boundaries you want to set. As you listen to your inner voice, you will notice when your boundaries are challenged. You will also be calmer when you need to express or enforce your boundaries.

I have found that it is hard to get angry with someone when they are calm and compassionate. When someone has disrespected my boundaries, I don't yell or start a fight. I calmly let them know I am uncomfortable with the situation.

An example of this happened recently. I was with friends, and one of them started to speak harshly about another friend of mine. I let her finish, and then I said, "I love you ____. I can hear you are frustrated, and you may have a reason to be. However, _____ is my friend, and I am uncomfortable talking about this behind her back. If you need to vent, I understand, but I am the wrong person."

Everything I said was true. This is very important: say true statements. I do love my friend, that is true. I am uncomfortable, that is true. She is allowed to vent, just not to me; that is true.

I can love someone and disagree with them. I can tell them I love them and ask them to honor my boundaries, assuming both are true.

As a recovering people-pleaser, it is easy to try to shape the truth to keep the peace. But one of the boundaries I hold myself to now is telling the truth even when it is contradictory and difficult.

A MEAL FOR ONE

SALMON WITH ZUCCHINI AND CARAMELIZED ONIONS

+

CHOCOLATE-COVERED STRAWBERRIES

I love this nourishing, easy meal for the nights when I need some love but I am also exhausted. You could make more servings, of course, but if you want to fill your cup, do not hesitate to cook for a party of one.

INGREDIENTS

One onion, thinly sliced
Generous amount of olive oil
1 to 2 zucchinis, chopped
Garlic clove, minced
A nice piece of salmon or halibut or whatever fish you like
Always, good salt and pepper

Fresh, ripe strawberries (This also works beautifully with pineapple.)
A handful of your favorite, high-quality chocolate chips

DIRECTIONS

Heat the olive oil to medium-high and add the sliced onions.

Stir occasionally and cook until they are brown and caramelized. This can take a while.

Add the chopped zucchini and sauté until it is cooked to your taste. (I like it a little browned.)

Add the garlic and stir until everything is done to your liking.

Heat another pan to high heat. Brush the fish with olive oil and sprinkle with salt and pepper to taste.

Once the pan is hot, place the fish flesh down on the pan to sear it and give you a nice crust.

When the fish is seared, turn it over, skin-side down, and put a little water in the pan. Cover with a tight lid, turn the heat to low and cook for about five minutes or until the fish is almost cooked through.

Take the fish off the heat and let it sit for a few minutes to finish cooking.

Prepare your decadent dessert:

Melt a handful of chocolate chips in the microwave in thirty-second bursts.

Let the chocolate cool slightly and stir to a frosting consistency.

Dip strawberries or pineapple.

Put the dipped fruit on a sheet of parchment paper and let it cool while you enjoy your dinner.

I highly recommend eating these delectable treats while watching reruns of Seinfeld.

Now get out a thank you note and send it to:

Kelley Wolf
2100 Park Ave. #681919
Park City, UT 84068.

CHAPTER 13
GRATITUDE & DIRT

Gratitude is your "Get out of jail free" card—it is the speed train to FLOW and the gateway to Love.

If you pay close attention whenever you feel love, you will notice that gratitude is sitting shotgun if it hasn't completely grabbed the wheel. And when we are in an anti-flow state—sitting in resentment, judgement, worry—we can use gratitude to get us back on track.

By now, you are aware that I have had deep traumas to overcome. I intentionally chose not to share my most devastating experiences here, because when you witness trauma, even from a distance, your body reacts. You may feel sadness, fear or anger—something from the menu of difficult feelings—alongside compassion and empathy.

My intention here has been to keep you in a place of relative lightness. Your energy matters in this journey, and my job is to hold it in good faith. Maybe a future book will tell the stories of overcoming, but not here, not today. Today, we stay right here, and that, my friends, is a beautiful place to be.

Today, if you assess life on tangible things like safety, financial security, family and health, I would tick all the boxes. My life is wonderful beyond my wildest dreams, and it keeps growing and flourishing in ways I never imagined.

Can you guess how hard it was for me to write those last sentences? It has taken me decades to own the truth of having a beautiful life. I always needed to play small. It seemed important to present myself as damaged and struggling. It's another quality of people-pleasers: "I am not a threat to you. Look how insignificant I am!"

I know now that this is a trauma response. Many of us jump on the struggle train to try and fit in.

Now, I want to yell it from the rooftop: "What a wonderful life!!"

Yet life is also complicated. It includes suffering, day in and day out.

No matter what our lives look like, rich or poor, sickness or health, single or married, kids or no kids, we all will have bad days. Terrible days of heartbreak and grief.

As you may have heard a thousand times before, the quality of our lives is determined by *how* we respond to the hard things. What they usually don't tell us is that we are hardwired to react with full-on fight/flight/freeze, so it isn't easy to respond in ways that invite peace. That's why we need a process like FLOW to keep us from staying stuck in catastrophic thinking, to help us take action on hard things instead of ruminating. FLOW can pull you towards gratitude when you struggle to see the silver lining.

I like to think of this on a scale: look at how you feel and rate it, from one to ten. One is almost blissful peace, and ten is full-blown rage. How do you feel when you experience frustrations? Make a mental note of your number as the day moves forward. I will caution you that living at around a seven or eight will make ten just one rude driver away. My goal is to roam around at two to four on any given day, which gives me room to experience hardship without falling off an emotional cliff.

Almost every morning, I take a hike. Hiking is my church. The trees are my best friends, and that daily walk is often my lifeline to a state of flow.

Yet on my hike a few days ago, I was angry as hell. My mind was clicking through frustrations like a court clerk. Not enough time in the day, everybody needs something, why am I so fried, why did we move, I hate this ... blah, blah, blah.

I was rolling in the mud like a champ.

Then I tripped. I almost fell face-first onto a jagged rock. I took a moment to center myself, and when I stood up, I knew what had just happened. My guides, my inner wisdom, spirit or an untied shoelace had tripped me right out of my anger spiral.

It was all I needed to wake me up. I took three deep breaths and then started listing the things I was grateful for.

My list always starts with walking because there was a time when future walking was not guaranteed for me. When I was first diagnosed with EDS, I learned that being in a wheelchair was one possible outcome. I can promise you, a shock to your system like that will remind you how much we take for granted.

Those of us with new reading glasses may add *seeing* to our gratitude list. As soon as I hit forty-two, I noticed I couldn't read the small print on the back of a yogurt container. Once I was sure I hadn't gotten lotion in my eye, I added vision to my gratitude list.

These things are not guaranteed. Isn't that powerful?

How often do you take your beating heart for granted? Do you assume your feet will carry you to the car? Oh, you have a car?

You see what I am saying?

As I walked, I kept going: the oxygen in the air, the trees, the smell of the ocean, my dogs, my car, my brain, my fingers that type this.

Stephen Hawking wrote some of the most profound works of literature of all time without being able to type. It is incredible what we are capable of, and it is also incredible what we can easily take for granted. As I listed what I was grateful for, my entire body shifted. I felt a warmth around me, I felt awake and alive, and I felt happy and inspired.

You, too, will notice a pronounced shift in your energy when you move your focus to gratitude. Even in the depths of despair, we can find at least one thing we are grateful for. It may be seeing or walking, or your car or your partner. Whatever you can find, say it in your head or write it down.

Do it now. Put this book down and notice the beauty that surrounds you, even if it is only the fact that you are here, breathing.

Life is hard. There is no such thing as a perfect life.

I have been lucky to hold space for many people from many corners of society and the world. I have yet to find someone who has not experienced suffering, but I believe we can minimize our internal strife. We can work on how we see and interpret the events that happen to us, but we will never avoid pain altogether.

This universal truth is why we must cultivate tools to help heal our lives, including gratitude. The alternative is to live without peace.

Focusing on gratitude is easily the most transformative thing I can do in a day. It requires nothing but a shift of the mind. Writing a list can be fun, but a simple nod to the sunrise can also have your day heading in a different direction.

Then there is the alternative, choosing to look at the world through a dirt-covered lens. Do you know someone who has committed to a life of resentments, cynicism and negativity? Is it you?

I will throw some tough love out here, but I must ask you—do you enjoy being with that person?

When we fall into the trap of resentment, we become a people repellent. It is like we have a cloak of funk around us.

I have had people sincerely ask me why no one wanted to spend time with them when the self-evident answer was that they chronically complained, gossiped, judged others, lived in chronic outrage and moaned about life.

It is hard to see our responsibility in managing our energy. We can believe we have a right to complain, to judge the mom who doesn't wave back in the pickup line. The reality is that surrendering to this negativity means that we are repelling positive people from our energy fields.

When I fall into that trap, and I do, I can see the effects in real time. Friends don't call. Invites don't come. I trip. Even when I have not said a word to the outside world, the universe knows that I am not in co-creation. I have stopped seeing the magic in life and become a "clod of grievances and ailments," as George Bernard Shaw wrote.

It's a reminder that it is time for me to reach for gratitude. Then I can begin to shift my energy.

As quickly as the universe trips me, it also rewards me for changing focus. It may be a phone call with good news or a roadside peach stand on my way home. Or maybe that peach stand was always there, and I just didn't see it because I was too busy complaining about the stain on my shirt.

All you need to know for sure is that gratitude is the quickest way to activate flow.

Start right here!

Go ahead and write in this book.

Start with three things you are grateful for right now.

NOT-YOUR-MOMMA'S EGGPLANT PARMESAN

NOT-YOUR-MOMMA'S EGGPLANT PARMESAN

Vegetarian, and No Frying

I show my appreciation with food. I am famous for showing up with a casserole instead of a bushel of flowers as a hostess gift. This recipe is one of the easiest takes on a universal favorite. It uses simple, fresh ingredients to create a dish worthy of gratitude.

INGREDIENTS

2 medium eggplants
Salt
3-4 tablespoons olive oil
One jar of good tomato sauce (Or homemade, if you please.)
1 mozzarella ball, thinly sliced
1 cup freshly grated parmesan[9]
About 10-12 torn basil leaves

DIRECTIONS

Preheat your oven to 375 F.

Lightly oil a casserole dish.

Slice the eggplant into 1/2-inch rounds. Sprinkle with salt and let sit. Water will bead on the top. (Magic!)

When the water drops stop forming, pat the rounds dry with towels.

Heat your broiler and broil the eggplant on each side until brown.

In a saucepan, warm the tomato sauce with the basil leaves.

Spread a third of the sauce on the bottom of the casserole dish.

Layer on eggplant, mozzarella and parmesan.

Add another third of the tomato-basil mixture, and again layer eggplant, mozzarella and parmesan on top. This will make two or three layers, depending on the size of your dish.

[9] Do not even try using dehydrated parmesan powder here. Others have suffered so you don't have to.

Bake until bubbling. If the top doesn't brown, pop it under the broiler to get a crispy, cheesy topping.

CHAPTER 14
MORE WAYS TO FIND FLOW IN YOUR LIFE

My husband is an actor who works out of town quite often. Our life together has been one of regularly saying goodbye to places, people and projects, but I am not complaining. I often find solace in my time alone with the kids and in exploring new places. It can be exhausting, but I relearn how strong I am every time I fly solo or make a new life in a new city for our family.

When Scott is away for work, I have an extra parking spot in my driveway. We recently moved to a house close to a public beach, and our street is always busy with people searching for that rare open parking spot.

When I need a little shot of flow, I sit on my front porch and wait for the car moving slowly down the block, hoping someone will leave and open a spot. My favorite is when the vehicle is full of kids, with a solo parent who would otherwise have to haul their gear from blocks away. I slowly walk to the window of their car and say, "You can park in our spot. There is no time limit."

I will never have the words to express how much impact small acts of kindness like this can have. It is truly remarkable. Usually, the parking spot winner will first think it is a prank. Then they realize it's not, and many people cry. It's just a parking spot, of course, but it is so much more. It is a remembrance of our connection to one another.

Any act of kindness, no matter how small, will leave an indelible mark that you cannot fully comprehend—on the giver and receiver, and possibly on others around you.

Let me share a story with you about a woman I once knew named Carol. She had become fiercely angry and felt the world was against her. She was isolated, alone and only felt power when hurting people. Her favorite form of vitriol was through the legal system. She liked to sue people. She liked to take her ex-husband to court for any tiny infraction. She sued the local coffee shop for "glass" in her bagel shmear. She had lots of money and lots of anger, and she used both to inflict pain on others.

Then Carol moved to a new neighborhood where no one knew her, and a neighbor named Alice invited her over for a barbecue. Carol was suspicious because she hadn't been invited anywhere for years.

Alice had no idea of Carol's background and was always open to meeting new friends. When she arrived at the barbecue, Carol was greeted with such warmth and genuine hospitality that she didn't quite know how to act. She had her best night in years, maybe even a decade.

When Carol got home, she had a message from Alice, thanking

her for coming and saying that she was looking forward to getting to know her more.

Alice didn't know that Carol had slipped coming up her driveway and was prepared to hate her new neighbors, even slap them with a lawsuit if she felt so inclined.

Instead, Carol realized something: she had become such a resentful person that she was pre-planning a way to hurt someone she barely knew, someone who was clearly kind.

Carol started to see the ways she had damaged lives. She decided then and there to begin to fix what she had broken. She revoked all the lawsuits she had in the works. She apologized to the coffee shop owner and paid for a new drive-through window for their business.

As Carol made these amends, she became addicted to the feelings it gave her. She became a new woman. She forgave herself and realized that her need to inflict harm came from past trauma. She committed to healing and became a source of healing for others.

All of this started because Alice offered one kindness to Carol, having her over for dinner.

You will never know what an act of kindness will do for someone and what ripple effects it might have. Imagine all the people who were positively affected by Alice's acts of kindness towards Carol.

Ultimately, the outcome of our kindness is none of our business. Our business is to act from love—when we see an opportunity to offer kindness, we take it.

As Maya Angelou once said, "When you know better, you do better."

You have probably guessed that my favorite acts of kindness usually involve food.

I had an elderly neighbor, a proud and lovely man with Parkinson's, who lost his wife to an aneurysm. He did not like asking for help, especially from a frazzled mom of three. So, I didn't give him the chance to ask. When I made dinner, I made an extra plate and sent the kids across the street to put it on his front step. Then I texted him to let him know.

We moved away, and when I went back to the neighborhood for a visit, I stopped by with a plate to leave on the step. He was sitting outside, and he began to sob. He couldn't stop crying. Finally, he put his hand on mine and said, "Thank you. You will never know what this has meant to me."

What he will never know is what it meant to me. Each time I experience the joy of giving, I can feel my heart expand. It sends warmth through my body. I feel connected and alive. I could even say these acts feel selfish because I get so much out of the experience.

I have many stories of the power of food. I have a simple rule: People need to eat. No matter what. If someone is going through something, never say, "What do you need?" When someone is struggling, they don't know what they need, but you do. At some point, they will need to eat. If you don't cook, grab a bag of oranges and some bagels and cream cheese. Order DoorDash or hire a caterer to drop off some soup or get a pizza delivered. This is easy: feed people and they will feel cared for.

I can remember every food item brought to me when I was in a bad way. Every. Single. One.

Even more exciting is dropping off a treat for no reason at all. Just randomly bring a bag of bagels and cream cheese to a friend's house. No explanation needed, just a little card that says, "I love you."

Can't you feel that?!

That is flow—that is how it feels.

KINDNESS LEMON BARS

KINDNESS LEMON BARS

A cherished recipe from the best chef I know, my mom Elaine Williams.

If you are ever going through a Carol moment—if you feel resentful and left out—break the chain and take someone these lemon bars. I promise the kindness will come back to you.

INGREDIENTS

Crust
2 cups flour
1/2 cup powdered sugar
1 cup softened butter

Filling
4 beaten eggs
2 cups sugar
1/3 cup fresh squeezed lemon juice
1/4 flour
1/2 teaspoon baking powder
1/4 cup powdered sugar (for topping)

DIRECTIONS

Preheat oven to 350 F.

Crust

Sift the flour and powdered sugar together.

Cut in the butter until the mixture feels like sand. My daughter Lucy and I do this together, and we squish the butter into the flour with our fingers until we get the right texture.

Press the crust into a buttered, 9" by 13" by 2" pan.

Bake for 25 to 30 minutes until the crust is lightly browned.

Filling

While the crust is baking, combine the eggs, sugar and lemon juice.

Beat well.

Sift the flour and baking powder together, and fold into the egg mixture.

Pour the filling over the lightly browned crust and put the pan back in the oven for 25 to 30 minutes.

When the bars have cooled, sift the powdered sugar over the top and then cut the whole delicious mess into squares.

RECIPE 2

In case you need more inspiration at this point, here are some small ideas that may lead to ... who knows what.

1. Take some lemon bars to the teachers at school.
2. Bring coffee to roadside workers.
3. Send a text to a friend that says, "You are making a difference and you are loved."
4. Donate $5 to any charity for no reason.
5. Let someone into traffic.
6. Leave a good review and comment on a podcast or blog post.
7. Leave a big tip for a small item, like a $5 tip for a coffee.
8. Tell a random stranger they glow and look happy.
9. Send your mom a cookbook, or, if she doesn't cook, another book you think she'd enjoy.

10. Remember birthdays.

11. Clean up trash as you go.

12. Take a newspaper and tea to an elderly neighbor. Trust me, they miss the newspaper.

13. Write a college freshman a letter of encouragement[10].

14. When you buy yourself a book, buy two and give one away.

15. Take an extra blanket or chair to a soccer game or concert and let someone use it.

16. Keep lollipops in your car for crying kids.

17. Smile and wave.

18. Pay a compliment and mean it.

19. Remind a friend of one of their best qualities.

20. Say, "I love you."

Add three more of your own:

____

____

____

____

____

____

____

[10] Scott received a letter from a family friend while he was in college studying finance. It said they'd always thought he "had something special" and could be on the screen. It prompted him to enroll in an acting class—and the rest is history.

CHAPTER 15

ANOTHER ANTI-FLOW: THE DANGER OF "OTHERNESS"

ANOTHER ANTI-FLOW: THE DANGER OF "OTHERNESS"

I recently read this in Ann Druyan and Carl Sagan's 1997 book, *The Demon-Haunted World, Science as a Candle in the Dark*:

"I have a foreboding of an America in my children's or grandchildren's time ... [when], our critical faculties in decline, unable to distinguish between what feels good and what's true, we slide, almost without noticing, back into superstition and darkness ..."

I encourage you to read the book. It is astonishing how accurately they predicted the future we're now living in.

You may see this as a strange turn in a book about FLOW, but please stay with me. I believe we are perilously close to an irreparable division, especially in America, and that Dr. Sagan and Ms. Druyan's fears have sadly come to pass. Through the sound bites they predicted in the next paragraph of the book, "we are fed an addictive cornucopia of misinformation and otherness."

Otherness is the idea that we are to be suspicious of others, to see them as against us and our values. We may even question their moral integrity and intelligence.

The practice of FLOW can allow us to begin to heal this illness spreading across humanity. It's one of the reasons that I knew I couldn't put off writing this book any longer.

Healing starts with noticing thoughts of otherness. They could fall into the category of worry: when we believe we are separate, we are worried. It may present as anger or fear—we feel attacked.

Your othering thoughts may feel righteous and accurate but, given a few minutes of examination, you will likely find some errors or unprovable ideas.

I am guilty of this in many ways. I often find myself standing on a soapbox of righteous conviction. When I challenge my beliefs, I find myself defensive: "Yes, but I am right!"

These days, I am challenging myself to be calm, open and compassionate. What I have found is nothing short of a miracle—connection and understanding. How 'bout them apples?

It's now rare to find a person who is not deeply committed to their beliefs, with little or no space to hear opposing views.

Sadly, when this happens, we not only lose the opportunity to influence someone else's opinion, if that's what we want, but we lose the connection we have or could have with them. Research[11] points to the difficulty of changing opinions with information unless trust and shared values already exist in the relationship. That applies whatever the source—we all have relatives who trust a TV channel's opinions more than that of their family members.

[11] "So You Want to Convince a Climate Change Skeptic," by Spencer Bokat-Lindell in The New York Times, is a good starting point if you'd like to learn more about this research. https://www.nytimes.com/2020/01/02/opinion/climate-change-deniers.html

"Call out culture" assumes that telling someone where they are wrong is the solution to wrong-headed thinking, but it only works if we trust the person calling us out and feel they respect us and share our values. Otherwise, it feels like an attack and only creates more division.

Wherever you can, focus on building trust first. Offer respect for the opinions of others, even those you disagree with. This is not the same as condoning their views. Rather, it is opening a space for genuine connection and growth. Find common ground. Get curious. Is there anything you agree on? This can be the beginning of reconciliation, or at least of some grace and understanding.

We can use the FLOW recipe when we find ourselves angry at a family member across the table because of their last vote for congress. When you find yourself in this headspace, use FLOW to first identify what is causing you to suffer. It is hard because our anger says something like, "My sister, of course!" But go further.

Spoiler alert: it is not your sister.

It may be a fear of separation or of loneliness. It may be fear that someone you love is embracing different values and moving away from you. Can you identify the deeper cause of your suffering?

Let's say the fear is worry about losing the family closeness you thought you had.

Sit in this discomfort for a moment. Allow it to be in your body. Notice where you feel it. Notice your mind's desire to combat the discomfort through otherness, putting up a wall of anger between you and your sister.

You are now in the Finding state. They are just thoughts. Remember that.

Once we have observed the source of our suffering, we will make another choice. We will walk Over the thought bridge.

In this scenario, the fear thought is, "I am worried I will lose the closeness I thought we had." We notice that our suffering is rooted in sadness; we feel alone with our values. We are mourning the closeness we felt until our family member acted in a way we feel is wrong.

Now, attempt to choose another thought, one based in love and gratitude.

"I am grateful I am here, at this moment, with my family.

I am grateful for my sister's epic sense of humor.

I am grateful for the meal we are sharing.

I love my ability to stay calm in the face of conflict.

It is okay to feel this discomfort and still love my sister."

Notice how you feel after going through these steps. Is your body calmer? Can you see your sister in a more forgiving light?

We want the people we care about to see the world as we do, but it is on us to manage the internal response we experience when they don't.

Think about the sorrow we could avoid if we used these tactics more often before the family table becomes the family battlefield. (We are all family, by the way.)

Set aside your rightness and see if you can allow your mind and body a calm space in which to prioritize connection and your values.

It may sound idealistic and possibly even naive. However, we must challenge ourselves for the sake of creating a fairer, more equitable world. Think about the leaders who have made great change through optimism and love, people like Gandhi, Martin Luther King, Jr. and Nelson Mandela. Were they naive? Or did they know something we do not, that the real and lasting shifts we all crave can only come from love?

GRANDMA LILLIAN'S POT ROAST

Invite some friends with differing views over for dinner. Make this meal and share it. Let's see what happens when we break bread together and challenge the otherness we feel.

When I was a kid, this was my favorite meal. When I came home from college, I always requested this pot roast. When I made it for the first time, I was shocked, because it might be the easiest celebration meal anyone could make.

If you can open containers and stir with a spoon, you can make this recipe. My mom must have been thrilled that I didn't choose Beef Wellington, ha! And when you make this for a tough crowd, you will have ample time to rest and meditate before your guests arrive.

INGREDIENTS

4-5 pounds pot roast
1 10 oz. can cream of mushroom soup
1 envelope onion soup mix
1 empty mushroom soup can of red wine
1 empty can of water
1 onion, chopped
2 cloves garlic, minced
1 bay leaf
1 teaspoon thyme
1 teaspoon basil
1-2 pounds sliced carrots
1-2 pounds potatoes (the little ones if you can find them.)

DIRECTIONS

Put the roast in an ovenproof casserole dish.
Combine all other ingredients.
Pour over the meat.
Add carrots and potatoes to the edges.
Cover tightly with foil.
Bake at 350 degrees F for 3 1/2 hours.
Stir veggies a couple of times while cooking.

CHAPTER 16

PROTECTING YOUR PEACE

In this chapter, we'll explore the FLOW version of boundaries. You may find this and the previous chapter in opposition, but I encourage you to think of the scales of justice, with these two concepts on either side. Our aim is to balance the scales—to stay open to connection without sacrificing ourselves.

We haven't yet talked about how much one peaceful person can change the energy of a family or even a community. To be that person, we must have boundaries that protect us from exhaustion and from absorbing too much of other people's energy.

When you begin your journey toward a more peaceful existence, you may feel overwhelmed by the energy around you. You may even feel judgement toward those you see as blind to their growth potential.

You will need a way to protect your peace when these feelings come up.

I was recently asked to return to New Orleans for a reunion show of our season of MTV's "The Real World." I was a cast member on the show in 2000. The series was a salacious effort at a social experiment: the concept was to choose seven people from varying backgrounds, put them all in a house for five months and film them as they learned to live together. The concept was fascinating, but the show tended to devolve into TV-worthy shenanigans. The season I was on seemed to stay aligned with its intention of confronting hard questions about society, however. One castmate was gay, one Mormon, one black, one interracial, one deeply Christian, one with an affluent family and an Ivy League education, and me, inaccurately described as "the southern belle, sorority girl."

Their description has always made me laugh. I was in a sorority for six months before I dropped out. I could see the benefits of the institution for many, but it was not for me. And the stereotypical "Southern Belle" couldn't be further from my ethos. I always felt like an alien in southern culture. My family originated in Indiana and moved to Arkansas when I was two years old, but we never acclimated to the grits and country music associated with southern living. We landed outside the norms of our community in everything from fashion choices to politics and most definitely religion or lack thereof.

Before New Orleans, I was living in the UK for a break from college, bartending. I met my boyfriend at the restaurant where we both worked, and we decided to take a trip to the island of Grenada before I left for the show. It was December of 1999, and in case the predictions of a Y2K mass technological breakdown proved to be accurate, we chose an off-the-grid house with no running water and fruit trees on the front lawn for easy breakfasts.

When I arrived in New Orleans and was labeled the "sorority-southern belle," I felt a sense of frustration even as I laughed at the assumption. I was far from the categories I'd been placed in, which is true for most humans on the planet.

When I got the call to do a reunion show, I had a wave of emotions, everything from shame to excitement. I watched my old season again and found myself in a tizzy over reentering this world, even though my adult brain knows we are all now middle-aged people and not hormonal teens and twenty-somethings.

When I noticed myself spinning in my fear about being in that space again, I noticed something else: I had forgotten my right to protect my peace. I was also fortune-telling, predicting future feelings of manipulation and subjugation.

I made a choice and followed the FLOW recipe, rediscovering many amazing, beautiful things that happened during that time or because of it. I came out the other side of the process with awe and a renewed appreciation for the magic of life.

Next, I turned my focus toward my power to protect my peace during the filming of the reunion show. Whatever assumptions that might be made about me, I do not need to own them or even give them any time. I have the choice to enter any situation with a firm grip on my sense of self and my ability to FLOW.

Libby Moore, who you read about earlier when she probably saved my life, taught me the following techniques to protect my peace. They work every time.

FIRST, BREATHING. SO SIMPLE. SO IMPORTANT.

Three deep breaths and slow exhalations.

Again.

Again.

Notice your body relaxing. Breathing is the most vital element of your peace. Even when you are not feeling overwhelmed, take some time out at the top of each hour for a few deep breaths.

BUBBLING

First, envision yourself in a situation you find uncomfortable. Next, envision a transparent bubble around you. This bubble doesn't separate you from others, but it keeps your energy with you and the energy of others with them. In your bubble, you will notice that you feel a sense of security. Bubbling allows you to be discerning about who and what you allow to influence you. If you are in a state of focus and flow, this exercise will enable you to maintain it even in the company of others.

ENERGY RETURN

This technique has genuinely changed my life. It is on the woo-woo side, but then so is the placebo effect, right? Something happens when you take the time to send energy home. After interacting with someone, take a moment to say, "Please send all the energy in my space back to its rightful owner and return my energy to me."

I have incredible interactions with my clients, but we often talk about heavy personal things. If I allowed all that energy to stay with me as I move from one conversation to the next, I would be a wreck, unable to do my best work. I would also inadvertently bring heavy energy to those it does not belong.

I just had a conversation with a fellow castmate from "The Real World." I called him from Whistler, BC, where I have come to write for a few days, and we immediately fell into past frustration and resentments we had about the series. I had been using all my tools for protecting my peace, and I started to tell him I did not want to live in negative energy, even though it is seductive. As we began to shift the conversation to possibility and the desire to be of service, a huge bear crossed the path I was walking on. A bear!

My mind was instantly laser-focused on trying to remember the safety protocol for bear encounters. I slowly backed up and then quickly ran down the trail back to the condo.

My heart was racing with fear, but also because I saw the significance of this interaction. In many spiritual traditions, the bear represents powerful, calm leadership, standing our ground and facing our deepest fears. Some traditions see the bear as a symbol of healing that allows us to be of service to others.

BOOM. I cannot make these things up.

When you begin to protect your peace, you will begin to see the power that comes from doing so. You are now drawing from an endless source of powerful energy, the energy of love.

You are love.

You are love. When you engage with the lie that you are not worthy, or you are not love, negative energy has an entry point. When you live in the understanding that love is your true nature, however, you'll find that the whole universe conspires to work in your favor.

ARUGULA SALAD WITH FLANK STEAK

ARUGULA SALAD WITH FLANK STEAK

Sometimes the best food is the simplest food. I wanted this recipe to be deeply nourishing and by far the easiest—easy enough to make when you lack the time or energy for a meal, but you don't want to order out.

INGREDIENTS

Arugula
Cherry tomatoes
Lemon
Salt
Olive oil
Parmesan (optional)
1-2 pounds flank steak

DIRECTIONS

Massage olive oil into the arugula.

Squeeze the juice of half a lemon over top and sprinkle with salt.

Top with parmesan petals if you like.

Cover the flank steak in olive oil and generously salt and pepper.

Heat a cast-iron skillet to high.

Sear one side of the flank, then the other.

Put it in a 400 F degree oven, or reduce the heat and cook on the stovetop, for a few minutes until the steak reaches desired doneness.

Let it sit for about ten minutes, then slice and place the slices on top of the salad.

I know. Almost too easy to believe.

CHAPTER 17

CIRCLES OF SERVICE

When we set out on our spiritual journey, we tend to consume certain traditions. Some people may read the Bible; some may take in every word of Joseph Campbell. The Alchemist comes to mind as a standard bedside table staple. Yet whatever teacher you look to, they will all guide you towards the power of a service-driven life.

All the great teachings came to the same conclusion—when we pursue a life of growth, we must also open ourselves to the power of service.

However, I think this message has been bumbled a bit, not by the great teachers but by us, the humans on the receiving end. The thing is, our current culture demands productivity and hustle at breakneck speed. I wish we could all unplug from the expectations, but if you are like me, you end up getting sucked in despite your best efforts to dial back the busy.

Many people I know and work with report being chronically exhausted; many have turned to medications to help them manage. I am an advocate for whatever works. If you work with your doctor and therapist and feel good about your plan, I am not here to argue the benefits of medication. I have used it throughout my life. But I do believe we deserve to have all the options on the table.

I sat down and created an alternative to service burnout, a system I call the Circles of Service. I aimed to create a memorable, doable way to monitor and strategize the way we engage with the endless pulls on our time.

Each one of the circles centers the next, larger circle. Inside the core circle is you. You are the heartbeat of this system. Without you, the whole thing falls apart.

The circles are in this order:

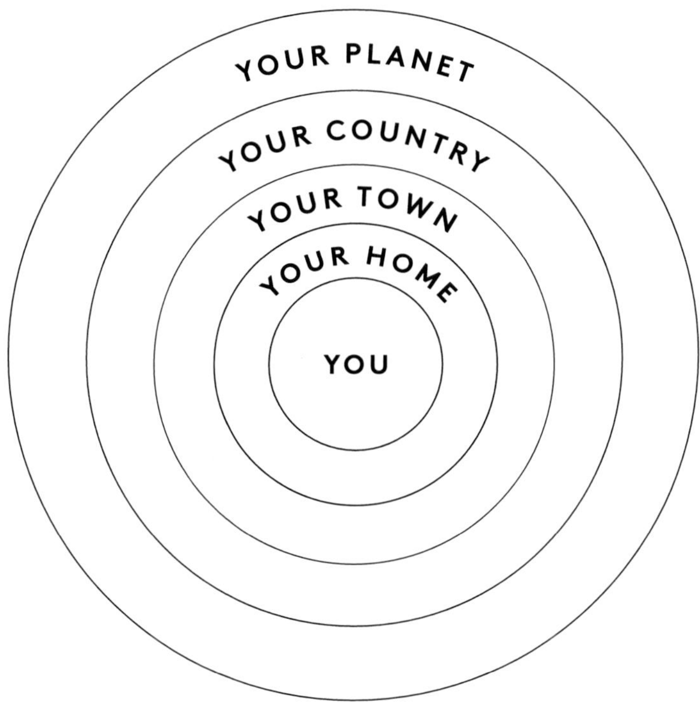
YOUR PLANET
YOUR COUNTRY
YOUR TOWN
YOUR HOME
YOU

I keep a copy of this diagram on my wall to remind me to check in. It helps me understand why I may sometimes feel resentful working at a volunteer station—it is always because I skipped at least one circle.

Living in flow requires serving ourselves first. To do this, first check in:

Are your needs being met?

Do you have judgements and resentments?

Are you chronically exhausted or chronically sick?

The mistake we often make is serving until we are empty and wondering if it is time to start Prozac. It may be—that is not my point. Sometimes we are not clinically depressed but have stopped listening to ourselves.

We need to gently turn up our own volume. Don't worry about why it's low—just find a quiet place to sit and turn it up until you hear that familiar beat only you can recognize. Once you do, tune in.

Ask some questions: "My love, how are you doing?" "What do you need right now?"

It may feel silly at first, but there is often a surprising response. A real response. It could be as simple as, "I am tired and need a nap," all the way to, "I don't feel safe and I need you to leave this situation."

It is possible we turned down the volume so we won't hear the scary truth of our heart's call. If you get an answer that feels insurmountable in the moment, you can respond with, "I hear you. I will help you. What can I do right now to start our process of healing?"

You may hear something like, "Cry."

This first circle is often the hardest because we tend to neglect it and jump to the next. I invite you to spend a fair amount of time here. You may need some extra attention—most of us do.

The next circle is your home. I use "home" instead of family because we all have different situations. Some people have kids, some do not. Some have animals, some do not. Some live with extended family members or friends. Some of us live alone, but our "home" is our small circle of chosen family. Whatever your story, you will have the energy and desire to be of service to those with whom you share your home after you have prioritized your own care.

You can see why we often skip circle one and jump to two. The whole world praises our care of our home circle. This is the circle of parenthood and tidy homes—people perceived as putting this circle before themselves are honored. I am most guilty of jumping to this circle over my own care. It has taken many years and much work to see the error in this choice. If our tank is empty, we are pouring from our reserves, and we will break down.

The next circle is your town or community. When you have served yourself and your home, and if you have time and energy left over, you can get curious about the needs of your community. It might be volunteering for school events or joining a civic group in your neighborhood. There are many options.

However, if you are exhausted, broke, sick, etc., it is not time to bring brownies for the bake sale but to circle back to circle one. I am repeating this because it bears repeating. I had a friend who ended up in the hospital because she spread herself so thinly her body shut down. The next time we went to a school meeting, I made her sit on her hands when they asked for parent volunteers. Her fear of being seen as lazy or a bad mom had literally sent her to the hospital! There are many seasons in our lives, and in some of them, you may not be able to serve outside your door. That's okay. There will be other seasons.

The next circle is your country. Remember John Kennedy's speech, when he said, "Ask not what your country can do for you but what you can do for your country." If you still have the bandwidth to do anything outside of your inner circles, I encourage you to look at the needs of your country. In this category, you may want to run for public office, donate to a national outreach like Feeding America, or just plan a road trip to underserved communities to support them with tourist dollars.

Whatever your desire, if you have the space for this level of service, then I believe you are called to do this work in a way many are not. When you get that call, you must heed it. Your service is needed.

The last circle is the planet. Reminder: service to each of the other circles will also benefit the planet. As we become more awake and engaged in our journey, we start to see the living world around us. We begin to care about the trees, the water, the sky and our impact on it all. A walk in the woods to fill your cup is also a moment your gratitude grows for the generous trees that provide us with oxygen and shelter. The moment you take to read a book might be the same moment you notice the plastic bottle you're drinking from and make the change to reusable.

It is very difficult to make positive change in our lives when we are stressed and overwhelmed. I once saw an article that showed a correlation between buying plastic cups and plates with overwhelm and exhaustion! Not surprisingly, we tend to choose the easiest path when we are depleted, and that is often the path of disposable dishes. Take a moment to consider this: when I am overtired, I will go to a drive-through or order take-out. Again, nothing against take-out, not even close. But when I make that choice, it comes with a lot of waste. When I have replenished myself, I might take a container to the restaurant and ask them to use it rather than single-use plastic. Granted, this is a rare occurrence in my life, and this is simplistic example. My point is that I am on to myself, and I will strive to do better every day I am given on this planet. Each day is a new opportunity to make better choices—and I make the best choices for me when my tank is full. Find Love Over Waste!! How about that?!

When you are in the planet circle, you can begin to think about what you want your service to provide to our planet. In this circle, the obvious one is the planet's health. A less obvious one may be a book you want to write, or another country you have hoped to support or a service or invention that could change the world.

Imagine being in a state of abundance, pouring service into the many needs of our world. To get there, start within.

FLOW VEGAN SOUP

I love putting vegan meals into my meal rotations. I always feel good when I eat a more plant-forward diet, and we cannot argue the benefits to the planet when we lessen our reliance on animal products—win-win. In the winter, I usually have this in my fridge because it tastes so good and is excellent brain food for gray days.

INGREDIENTS

Olive oil
1 onion, diced
2-3 carrots, diced
A few celery stalks, diced
A few potatoes, diced (Substitute or add canned beans or lentils if you'd like more protein.)
3-4 cloves of garlic, minced
28 oz. can of diced tomatoes
1/2 cup white wine (optional)
Fresh tarragon (Or 1/2 teaspoon dried tarragon)
White pepper
Salt and pepper
Veggie broth to taste

DIRECTIONS

Heat the olive oil in a soup pan until it shimmers.

Sauté the onions, celery and carrots. (I like mine lightly browned.)

Add the diced potato (or beans or lentils) and sauté for a moment. The potatoes will cook in the broth; this is just a little scoot around the pan.

Add the garlic and sauté until you can smell it cooking.

Add the chopped or dried tarragon, a pinch of white pepper and salt and pepper. Be generous with the salt and pepper:

maybe 1 1/2 teaspoon salt and 3/4 teaspoon of pepper? You can skip this if you'd like but it does add pop to the flavor.

If you wish, add the white wine to the veggies. Let the wine cook down until it is very minimal.

Now add the tomatoes. Stir and sauté for a moment.

Add the veggie broth.

Let simmer for about 30 minutes before serving.

This is a very flexible soup and you can get creative in terms of additions.

I like to serve this with bread and cashew butter. Scrumptious!

CHAPTER 18
FINDING LOVE WHEN LIFE FEELS UNBEARABLE

My mission is to constantly strive for a flow state by using the FLOW recipe. When I do, I live from a place of abundance and gratitude. In this state, there is no such thing as lack. I see all things as a part of the process and an opportunity to grow.

I have experienced profound trauma in my life. Like most of us, I have had many heartbreaking and devastating experiences throughout my time on this beautiful planet, and as I promised before, I won't travel down those roads here. This book is about maintaining love and lightness of being even as we face challenges.

When people ask me about applying FLOW when things are very hard, I think back to the challenges in my life. Would this path have served me when I didn't want to go on? Or would I have seen this as hyperbole?

This is how I answer that question: Suffering will always be the one thing we can count on. It always has been. It has been endured since the beginning of time, and great atrocities are happening somewhere on this planet even as I type these words.

My friends from Sudan walked across their country after-witnessing the genocidal murder of their families. A dear friend of mine lost her three-year-old daughter in a choking accident. One of my friends endured sadistic beatings from her abusive husband for years before she got away.

Pain, trauma and suffering are part of the human experience. Is it possible to FLOW when you are escaping a war-torn country? How can you munch, move and meditate when you have no food to eat?

These are the questions I asked myself as I wrote each word. My answer is, I believe it is the only way. No matter the level of suffering, we must believe in the power of Love to guide us forward.

The overtired mom, the stressed-out CEO and the wrongfully imprisoned human rights advocate are all capable of tapping into the power of love. We have a deep source memory of what it means to feel love. Even if we are utterly alone, wracked by trauma, and despair has set in, we can still access love. And love can save us.

I will offer you the wisdom of my friend Jiel, who is one of the "Lost Boys of Sudan," one of about twenty-two thousand boys separated from their families or orphaned during the Sudan Civil War[12].

In 2007, I was the co-founder of a nonprofit called the Chier Foundation, dedicated to funding education for Lost Boys and Girls living in Utah. (Chier is the North Star in Dinka; we asked the boys and girls we served to choose the name.) It was something we believed we could accomplish, and we did. In the process,

[12] 1987 to 2005

I learned something that forever changed how I look at the world.

Jiel is a very tall man with a smile that could light up the sky. He was seven when he came home from tending his cattle to find that his entire family had been slaughtered in their homes. Jiel and his fellow survivors began a trek that took them across Sudan and eventually to a refugee camp in Kenya. Along the way, these children, most between the ages of five and twelve, were attacked by lions and shot at by militias. Some died of starvation.

What he and the other kids endured is impossible for me to imagine.

One day, I asked Jiel if he was angry. I asked him how he had such a positive attitude.

He told me that time wasted in hate and anger is his time. "No one else will feel that suffering except for me. My rebellion is happiness. No one can kill my spirit. I choose to live in love, not hate."

Jiel went on to get his MBA from the University of Utah and is now working to build communities in his home country. He achieved his goal, and he continues to be one of my greatest inspirations. He is a light. He is *flow.*

Let happiness be your rebellion.

CHAPTER 19
MAGIC & ENERGY

I've saved this story for the end. If you have made it this far with me, we are now in this together. We are committed to waking up to the possibilities that life has in store for us.

After I came up with the recipe for FLOW, I was ecstatic. I was intrigued to see if I could live by my own words and what they would create.

Flow was a destination I craved, like all of us. I loved being in that unbounded feeling. I had felt it skydiving, in kisses and through achievement. I felt flow in my creative life as well, moments of time when time disappeared and I felt no angst. I felt present and enthralled. It is the most pristine state of being I have ever felt. The idea that there could be a guide to more of that feeling landed like a revelation.

I was sitting at my desk in a state of flow, writing up FLOW as a system. How could it be explained? Would people understand what I was sharing? It was so easy, and yet so hard to translate at first.

I started questioning and second-guessing myself. How could something so simple feel so powerful? Was I overreaching? Who did I think I was?

Then I saw it. FLOW is WOLF spelled backwards. WOLF is my last name. I had to look at it a few times to be sure. How had I never seen this? I felt dizzy with magic. It felt like this discovery was destined and I was in full alignment with my purpose. I felt flow.

I often talk about something I call the "breadcrumbs of your life." I have read this metaphor in books and heard it from colleagues; I am far from the first to use it. Breadcrumbs are little magic moments, conversations, meetings or incidents that help guide your course. They may show up in startling synchronicity. They may show up in the form of an animal sighting or a piece of garbage left on the ground with the exact symbol you needed to see—or the perfect anagram.

To believe in breadcrumbs, you need to believe in a little bit of magic, the kind we cannot explain. A hundred butterflies showing up to your wedding or a storm that canceled a trip that would have left your house to burn down from an electrical fire. (All breadcrumbs I have been told over the years.)

One of my favorite breadcrumb stories is the one about meeting my husband. I was living in New Orleans in an unhealthy relationship when I was asked to go to Mexico to film another show for MTV, the "Real World/Road Rules Challenge." I had sworn off reality TV, and I was conflicted, but I decided to go with the caveat that I would ask the other teams to vote me off first. That way, I would get paid for my participation, I could have a fun trip to Mexico, and I wouldn't have to be on the show.

I arrived in Mexico, and we filmed the opening sequences. I planned to share my request with the group that night at dinner, but in the afternoon, the producer came to our house and calmly said we needed to move to a safer area—a hurricane was about to hit the coastline.

It was the most devastating hurricane the area had experienced in over fifty years. The electricity was knocked out, bridges tumbled, and we were told to shelter in place. For two weeks, food and water were rationed, and we waited. We began to bond. We were no longer competitors; we were just a bunch of people trying to ride out a storm and survive. I fell in love with the people around me. We told stories over candlelight at night, played music, told jokes and drank the plethora of tequila that seemed to have survived the storm.

When it was time to start filming, I didn't want to go home. I decided to change my plan and let this play out. There was just one thing—I was the smallest, weakest person in the cast. I had not planned to compete, and now I was going up against professional athletes.

The first competition was called Vertical Limit, a climb up a 150-foot rope using buoys attached every five feet. I had never climbed a rope, and I watched the most athletic people in the group barely make it. When it was my turn, I took a deep breath and hoped not to look foolish. Instead, I climbed the entire rope, straight up. I beat everyone. Even the camera operator sat with his mouth gaping open. What just happened?!

That win moved my teammate and me to the top of the leader board and there we stayed until, by what seemed a miracle, we won the entire show.

We each won fifty thousand dollars. I was twenty-three-years old.

After returning to New Orleans, I knew I had to leave my relationship. I felt strong and inspired, but where would I go? I had always dreamed of living in New York City, so I called a friend I had met during filming who lived there. He said he could help me find a job and an apartment.

I found an apartment on Craigslist, and I arrived in New York on October 1, 2001, three weeks after the attack on the World Trade Center.

I'd decided to go despite the attack—like so many of us, I did not want evil to win.

I used a map to find my new address and took the subway from the airport. John Street—I saw the name and I was pumping with excitement. I exited the subway with only my backpack and the clothes I had on my back.

As I walked out of the station, I was hit with a giant plume of smoke. The rancid smell of burning metal and decay was overwhelming, and my body heaved from the onslaught. I was standing at the base of what had been the twin towers. With tears in my eyes, I looked for a street sign through the smoke. My new apartment was one block from ground zero. I was humbled and shaken, but I put my shoulders back and pressed on.

After living in New York for a year, the friend I had made on the MTV show said he wanted to introduce me to someone, his friend Joel Goldman. Joel was the celebrity liaison for the Elizabeth Glaser Pediatric Aids Foundation, and they wanted me to host college events to raise money for the foundation. I immediately loved Joel, and we traveled together to a few campuses where I spoke to students about EGPAF. One day Joel called me and said, "I want to set you up with my friend Scott." I asked a few questions, but I trusted Joel and said I would love to.

A month later, I got a call from Scott. He called me at four in the afternoon, and, if you knew me in 2002, you knew that I never talked to anyone during the Oprah Winfrey Show. That was sacred time. I quickly picked up the phone and said, "Could you call me back in an hour? I am watching Oprah."

Scott giggled and called back an hour later. The first thing he said was, "Can you believe what that woman went through?"

Yes, ladies and gentlemen, he is a good one. He watched the show, and that was it for me. I was in.

On our first date, I was forty-five minutes late because I couldn't get a cab and ended up being dropped off by a group of Wall Street bankers in a white limo. That is a whole other story for a whole other book. Scott waited, and you know the rest.

The breadcrumbs abound in this story. One after the other. Acts of God and little moments, all guiding me along my path.

Sure, there are rational, boring ways to explain these phenomena, but I want to believe in a little bit of magic. I choose to believe in a little bit of magic because my energy and the world around me sparkle a little bit more when I do.

When I am in full consciousness, I see breadcrumbs everywhere. I see magic all around me. Even when something is hard, I can feel the magic guiding me along—it's part of a FLOW life.

I make the choice to observe the world in a benevolent light.

You can too.

CHAPTER 20

NO ENDINGS, JUST NEW CHAPTERS

You have come to the end of the book, and I have come to the end of writing it. I like to picture you sitting on your favorite chair, eating a peanut butter ball or a lemon bar and maybe sipping some coffee.

I picture you with a little smile. The kind of smile that knows something, that gets the joke or knows the ending. It's a cheeky smile. Because somewhere in your heart, you know you have got this.

You know you are going to be okay. In fact, you know you are going to be better than okay. You know that you deserve a beautiful life. You know that this is your one shot, and you aren't going to sit on the sidelines and wait for someone to ask you to dance. You will hit that dance floor and make a damn fool of yourself because you are the embodiment of Love!

Whenever I doubted myself and my "right" to write, I thought of this moment—the one in which you and I share something this special, this powerful.

We know we can FLOW, and because we have the recipe, we also have the key to living in a blissful, timeless state of flow, whatever is going on around us.

We know that it doesn't matter what the naysayers say. We know that we can overcome any obstacle. We know that no matter what anyone says or what your mind may tell you, you are not what has happened to you.

We can rewrite our story each day when we wake up. Today—today is the day, my friend.

Today is the day you choose you.

You choose life.

You choose love over worry.

You choose FLOW.

And then,

you *flow.*

ACKNOWLEDGMENTS

ACKNOWLEDGMENTS

I first have to thank Nathaniel Rateliff for writing his song Redemption. Whenever I felt a block, I would put his song on repeat and the words would flow. Thank you Mr. Rateliff.

Next, Megan Watt, who gave me clarity and showed me the way forward. Megan, you aren't just a fashion icon—you helped me to see what is possible and, for that, I thank you.

Then I had my first book date with my editor, Lori Bamber. Lori is special. I knew it the first time we spoke. She walked in the park while we talked on the phone, and I am pretty sure I cried. I could feel it. She was the one. I have no doubt I tested Lori's patience when it came to my "magical thinking," but she persevered, and she deserves equal credit for the beauty of this book. Lori, I often picture you walking through the woods, "holding this book in [your] mind," watching out for potholes, looking for repetition and all the while making sure the magic never leaves the page. You are a rare find, my dear. I will live in gratitude for all my days.

I am not a designer, something I said many times to Stephanie MacDougall. Luckily, she is, and she spent hours calmly working and re-working as my clarity shifted. What she created is beyond my wildest expectations. Thank you, Steph.

Jessica Riesenbeck has been my cheerleader and my granny with a ruler: "Kell, it's time. We need to do this." Jess, thank you. You helped carry me to and over the finish line. Thank you.

So that is the book. Then there is a life, the life that happens while you are writing a book. The friends and family who wait for you to get back to them and patiently tap on the door when you have asked for "total solitude."

My family. My Wolf Pack. Man, do I love you. It sometimes hurts I love you so much. Lucy's taps at my door: "Momma, can I have a hug?" Miller runs through the door and leaps into my arms for his signature koala hug; Jackson stands behind the door and says, "Guys, Moms is working." (Me saying, "You better get over here and give me a hug, too!")

Then the big dog, the poppa wolf, Scotty, smiling, that twinkle ... oh that twinkle. Say it with me: "Give me a hug!" I love you, Scott Wolf. I love you to my bones.

I will hug you all to the end of my days even when you try and push me away. You are the flow beneath my wings. I love you. Always.

Mom and Dad—don't worry, I was listening. I was watching. You taught me every word in this book. Love will guide us through, and your love has always shown me the way. I love you.

My friends. I had to make a choice to say, "You know who you are." My ride or dies, my midnight calls, my walkers in the woods, my cactus friends, my new and my old, my panicked call from the pick-up line friends, my "I need your thoughts on this" and especially, my "Did we really say yes to this?" friends. I freaking love you. I love you so hard. You make it all work. Thank you ... forever and always.

And then there is you. If you read this book, then we did this together. We locked arms for the hours you gave to me and for that I am deeply grateful. Thank you for your time and your open heart. I may see you one day, and we won't know but we will know. We will know that we FLOW.

ABOUT THE AUTHOR

"I always wondered if Kelley married me for my last name—now I know for sure! FLOW is WOLF spelled backwards."

Scott Wolf, Husband, Father, Golden Globe-winning actor.

Kelley Wolf is a certified life coach who holds a degree in Clinical Psychology from Westminster College. She has had a thriving private practice for over a decade and worked with hundreds of individuals and companies to challenge thoughts and use FLOW to change the patterns of their behavior.

She is an avid traveler and has lived around the globe. She began her career in television and continues to work for major outlets like Viacom CBS and Paramount Plus. Kelley grew up in the beautiful hills of Northwest Arkansas and has moved more than twenty times. She currently resides in Vancouver, British Columbia, with her husband and three kids, where she is committed to munching, moving and meditating each day.

Made in United States
North Haven, CT
29 April 2022